100 Great Business Ideas

From Leading Companies Around the World

Jeremy Kourdi

CYAN

Marshall Cavendish
Business

Copyright © 2008 Jeremy Kourdi

First published in 2008 by:

Marshall Cavendish Limited
Fifth Floor
32–38 Saffron Hill
London EC1N 8FH
United Kingdom
T: +44 (0)20 7421 8120
F: +44 (0)20 7421 8121
sales@marshallcavendish.co.uk
www.marshallcavendish.co.uk

and

Cyan Communications Limited
Fifth Floor (Marshall Cavendish)
32–38 Saffron Hill
London EC1N 8FH
United Kingdom
T: +44 (0)20 7565 6120
F: +44 (0)20 7565 6121
sales@cyanbooks.com
www.cyanbooks.com

A CIP record for this book is available from the British Library

ISBN-13 978-1-905736-07-2
ISBN-10 1-905736-07-X

Designed and typeset by Curran Publishing Services, Norwich, UK

Printed and bound in Great Britain by
CPI Bookmarque, Croydon CR0 4TD

Contents

Acknowledgments

This book is the result of the support and encouragement of several people, and whilst the execution, style, and shortcomings are my own, their expertise and help must be acknowledged. Thanks go to Louise Kourdi, whose diligent research has been especially valuable, and Martin Liu and his talented colleagues at Cyan, whose patience, energy, and expertise is much appreciated.

Also, I have been very fortunate to work with some of the most stimulating, professional, and exceptional businesses, several of which are featured in this book. I owe a huge debt to all my clients and past employers who have, without doubt, provided the most interesting and exciting environments in which to work, learn, and develop.

Finally, my gratitude goes to my wife Julie and son Tom, for their constant support, encouragement, and inspiration.

Jeremy Kourdi

Introduction

This is a book about some of the best ideas used in business. Some are simple – sometimes almost embarrassingly so – while others are based on detailed research and brilliant intellect. Most are perennial, as their logic, simplicity, or value will help them endure; while others are, to be honest, rather faddy. What unites these business ideas is their proven power and potency. They are not only insightful and useful, they have worked: often in a brilliant way or despite great adversity. The ability of the people that conceived and applied these ideas should be applauded.

One word of warning: while these ideas have worked for the companies mentioned at the time they applied them, it is not to say that these businesses will always get everything else right, forever more. They produced a result at the time, but if this book has any general lessons it is that new ideas and energy are needed constantly – in many ways and at varying times – to ensure success.

While these ideas are varied and, I hope, interesting and thought-provoking, it seems to me that there are several different themes that run through many of these ideas and the businesses that use them. These include a willingness to experiment and take a risk. This seems to happen because many of the businesses display energy and entrepreneurship – a restless desire to do well and stay ahead of the competition. This is often coupled with an ability to understand the root causes of an issue, opportunity, or challenge, and do something distinctive, rather than merely tinkering with the status quo. Simplicity and an understanding of the need to be practical and implement the idea are also common features. Some ideas, however, do result from extensive study and research. This seems to confirm Peter Drucker's point that great ideas and decisions are a blend of rigorous analysis and intuition. Clearly, sometimes one aspect is more important (depending on the idea), but both are significant. Finally, the need to be practical, follow through, and ensure success is shown by the recurring need to monitor, measure, and refine the way the idea works.

A word of guidance: if you are thinking of applying these ideas in your organization it may help to understand a little of the way that ideas are transmitted. Ideas tend to be passed on either by "blueprint copying," which takes the whole idea and all its details and then replicates it elsewhere, or by "idea stimulation," where the details are unknown or adapted but the gist of the idea is applied. For example, in his excellent award-winning book *Guns, Germs, and Steel: A History of Everybody for the Last 13,000 Years*, Jared Diamond cites the development of an alphabet as an idea that arose independently probably only once and was then copied elsewhere. Of course, these techniques are opposite ends of a spectrum, but of the two methods, idea stimulation is surely more adaptable, robust, and likely to succeed. So, use these ideas to stimulate your thinking and make the specific adjustments needed to ensure success in your situation.

I hope that these ideas will provide you with the inspiration to find out more or develop your thinking along new, creative lines, generating brilliant ideas for the future.

Jeremy Kourdi

Please note that the ideas outlined in this book are listed randomly, for interest, rather than being grouped or ranked in a specific order.

IDEA 1
Building customer trust and loyalty

Both selling and influencing suffer from the similar misconception that success requires you to aggressively or cleverly push a product or idea. This misunderstanding leads to inappropriate behaviors. For example, people can become evasive, "pushy," and aggressive, or overly talkative and agreeable. Selling and influencing depends on getting behavior right, by moderating openness and assertiveness with warmth and competence. Combined with a great product or brand, this goes a long way to building customer loyalty.

The idea

Harley-Davidson overcame a turbulent past by building customer loyalty – one of its most enduring assets. It was one of the USA's foremost motorbike manufacturers but, by the 1980s, sales fell dramatically following tough competition from affordable, high-quality Japanese machines. Harley-Davidson improved quality using the production techniques of Dr. W. Edwards Deming. The next challenge was to win back, and maintain, market share (it now enjoys a customer loyalty rate of 90 percent).

Knowledge of customers' needs and appealing to customers'

emotions helped Harley-Davidson to build trust and bond with customers. Their managers meet customers regularly at rallies, where new models are demonstrated. Advertising reinforces the brand image, to promote customer loyalty. The Harley Owner's Group (HOG) is a membership club that entrenches customer loyalty, with two-thirds of customers renewing membership. Significantly, Harley-Davidson ensures customers receive benefits they value.

The result is that customers trust Harley-Davidson; this trust is used to develop stronger bonds and greater profits in a virtuous circle. Rich Teerlink, former chairman, commented, "perhaps the most significant program was – and continues to be – the Harley Owners Group (HOG)... . Dealers regained confidence that Harley could and would be a dependable partner... . [And] capturing the ideas of our people – all the people at Harley – was critical to our future success."

In practice

- Deliver customers a consistent (and ideally a "branded") experience each time they deal with your business.

- Be clear about the value proposition – what you are offering customers.

- Provide incentives for new customers to return and reorder.

- Reward loyalty for established customers.

- Be competitive – what seems like a good deal to you may not match your competitors.

- Make the customer's experience as easy and enjoyable as possible.

- Reassure customers with a reliable service and product offer.

- Continuously improve the process, based on customer feedback.

- Deliver reliability by working with partners and investing in resources.

IDEA 2
Scenario planning

Scenario planning enables organizations to rehearse the future, to walk the battlefield before battle commences so that they are better prepared. Scenarios are not about predicting future events. Their value lies in helping businesses understand the forces that are shaping the future. They challenge our assumptions.

The idea

In the 1960s, Pierre Wack, Royal Dutch/Shell's head of group planning, asked executives to imagine tomorrow. This promoted sophisticated and responsive strategic thinking about the current situation, by enabling them to detect and understand changes. Pierre Wack wanted to know whether there were other factors in the supply of oil, besides technical availability, that might be uncertain in the future. He listed stakeholders and questioned the position of governments in oil-producing countries: would they continue increasing production year on year? By exploring the possible changes to government policy, it became apparent that these governments were unlikely to remain amenable to Shell's activities. Many oil-producing countries did not need an increase in income. They had the upper hand, and the overwhelming logic for the oil-producing countries was to reduce supply, increase prices, and conserve their reserves.

When the 1973 Arab–Israeli War limited the supply of oil, prices rose fivefold. Fortunately for Shell, Wack's scenario work meant

Shell was better prepared than its competitors to adapt to the new situation – saving billions of dollars, it climbed from seventh to second place in the industry's profitability league table. It knew which governments to lobby, how to approach them, where to diversify, and what action to take with each OPEC member.

Scenario planning enables leaders to manage uncertainty and risk. Above all, scenarios help firms to understand the dynamics of the business environment, recognize new opportunities, assess strategic options, and take long-term decisions.

In practice

- Scenarios are not predictions: they are used to understand the forces shaping the future. What matters is not knowing exactly what the future will look like, but understanding the general direction in which it is moving – and why.

- Plan and structure the scenario process: for example, by agreeing who will be involved.

- Discuss possible futures (usually by working back from a possible view of the future).

- Develop the scenarios in greater detail.

- Analyze the scenarios: why they might occur, what you would do if they did.

- Use the scenarios to shape decisions and priorities.

IDEA 3
Making your employees proud

A company with a positive self-image and sense of pride will be more unified and efficient, with a stronger "employer brand." When employees respect and appreciate the organization they work for then their productivity, quality of work, and job satisfaction increase.

The idea

Are your employees proud of working for your business? This sense of pride may result from the organization's purpose, success, ethics, the quality of its leadership, or the quality and impact of its products. An example of this is Taylor Nelson Sofres (TNS), a leading market information company, with over 14,000 full-time employees across the world. It collects, analyzes, and interprets information for clients, provides research on business and market issues, and conducts social and political polling.

The firm's network spans 70 countries, and has been largely assembled through acquisition. Consequently, employees were often more loyal to their local "in-country" TNS business than to the group, which seemed remote or foreign. However, when one of its executives was caught in the tsunami in South Asia, in December 2004, TNS donated $250,000 to UNICEF to aid relief operations. This altruism brought the company together, as employees were pleased to be working for an organization with values that they respected.

As TNS illustrates, simple and positive gestures can achieve impressive results in terms of employee satisfaction, pride, and motivation.

In practice

- Carry out acts of corporate social responsibility – such as donation, fundraising, or simply enacting more compassionate business practices. These all serve to make current and potential employees feel proud to work with your organization.

- Ask employees what they value – what would they like their employer to do?

- Provide opportunities for employees to engage in fundraising and volunteering activities.

- Avoid negative business practices. Employees will be less motivated to work within an organization that is viewed negatively in society.

- Remind employees of the ways their services benefit society; how the everyday tasks they perform make a positive difference within society.

IDEA 4
Using customer information

Seamlessly gathered information can be used to save costs, to provide a tailor-made service to individual clients, and to sell more – often using the internet.

The idea

The US-based online retailer Amazon.com has redefined book-selling. Its culture appreciates the potential of technology, with the company using information in four key ways:

1. *To minimize risks* by analyzing information from millions of customers to see how and when they purchase, enabling Amazon.com to reduce the level of risk.

2. *To reduce costs* by using technology to control the way it manages its inventory and suppliers.

3. *To add value and help customers* by offering reviews of books and free downloadable information, and by treating its home page as an individual shop front for each customer – for example by tailoring lists of suggested titles that the customer may enjoy based on previous purchases.

4. *To innovate.* Amazon believes that to rival its competitors, an

innovative approach is essential in order to improve the value and service offered to consumers.

What matters is not simply what information exists, but *how* that information is used to build competitive advantage. Interestingly, many other retailing companies have now followed Amazon's lead. For example, Apple's iTunes and iStore have done for music retailing what Amazon did for bookselling, using many of the same principles.

In practice

- Treat each customer as an individual. For example, music retailer iTunes tracks the purchases of individual clients and provides a customized webpage designed to introduce a client to new buying opportunities that appeal to his/her personal taste.

- Use the internet to provide information for the individual – even if your business does not carry out its primary operations online. By collecting customers' email addresses, a business can develop a highly valuable and intimate marketing strategy.

- Smaller businesses and freelance workers may be able to research more in-depth information on each client. This can then be organized into an accessible database, with subheadings for each client covering all areas of relevant information.

- If your organization is unable to seamlessly track consumer trends, use incentives such as free products for customers that volunteer their information. Similarly, you should also provide rewards for customers that agree to receive information on your organization – the marketing should be entertaining, lively, appropriate, and relevant.

IDEA 5
The rule of 150

Coworkers find socializing, teamworking, and associated activities (such as innovating, collaborating, and sharing knowledge) much easier to achieve when they are placed in groups of less than 150. In this way, larger corporations gain the benefit of smaller groups that are often closer, more energetic, entrepreneurial, supportive, and better.

The idea

A fascinating example of an organization that clearly understands the benefits of collaboration is Gore Associates, a privately held, multi-million-dollar high-tech firm based in Delaware. As well as manufacturing the water-resistant Gore-Tex fabric, the firm also produces products for the semiconductor, pharmaceutical, and medical industries.

Gore is unique because of its adherence to the rule of 150. This approach is based on anthropological research highlighting the fact that humans can socialize in large groups because, uniquely, we are able to handle the complexities of social arrangements. However, there is a limit to the bonds people can make, and this is reached at around 150. In groups larger than 150, complicated hierarchies, regulations, and formal measures are needed, but below 150 these same goals can be achieved informally.

Consequently, Gore limits the size of each office so it is below 150. Gore has 15 plants within a 12-mile radius in Delaware and Maryland, each with a close-knit group of employees who understand each other and work well together. This approach emphasizes the benefits of collective management such as communication, initiative, and flexibility, and it has enabled a big business with thousands of employees to retain the attitude of a small, entrepreneurial start-up. The result is a rate of employee turnover that is a third of the industry average, and sustained profitability and growth for over 35 years.

In practice

- Divide your workforce into groups or branches of under 150 people.

- Institute a strong managerial system to oversee smaller "branches" and ensure they are coordinated and efficient.

- Encourage a sense of community and teamwork within groups. The "rule of 150" simply means that it will be possible for workers to form positive bonds with all of their coworkers – extra measures should be taken to ensure that this actually happens.

- Develop a sense of team across groups of 150. This means finding ways for people to communicate and collaborate across the whole business, rather than developing a series of competitive, separate groupings.

IDEA 6
Information orientation

Given that billions of dollars are invested each year in IT software and hardware, we might expect managers to know exactly how information technology improves their organization's results. Exactly what is the connection between the billions invested annually in IT, and improvements in productivity and performance? Information orientation has the answer – the three things that connect IT with business results.

The idea

Professor Donald Marchand together with William J. Kettinger conducted research at IMD business school that identified three critical factors driving successful information use. These three capabilities contain 15 specific competencies.

The three "information capabilities" combine to determine how effectively information is used for decision making:

1. *Information behaviors and values.* This is the capability of an organization to instill and promote behaviors and values for effective use of information. Managers need to promote integrity, formality, control, transparency, and sharing, while removing barriers to information flow and promoting information use.

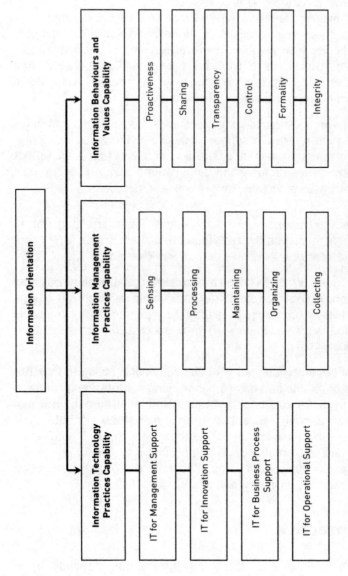

Diagram: the Information Orientation Maturity Model (source: Professor Donald Marchand)

2. *Information management practices*. Managing information involves sensing, collecting, organizing, processing, and maintainance. Managers set up processes, train their employees, and take responsibility for the management of information, thereby focusing their organizations on the right information. They take care to avoid (or at least minimize) information overload, improve the quality of information available to employees, and enhance decision making.

3. *Information technology practices*. IT applications and infrastructure should support decision making. Consequently, business strategy needs to be linked to IT strategy so that the infrastructure and applications support operations, business processes, innovation, and decisions.

Several companies have successfully implemented major IT projects, including Banco Bilbao Vizcaya Argentaria (BBVA) and SkandiaBanken, Sweden's first branchless bank.

BBVA transformed its failing branch-based retail banking business into one of the most successful banks in Spain within 1,000 days. This was accomplished by getting the right information to people in the branches, enabling them to successfully cross-sell their products.

SkandiaBanken created a model for online business that has been profitable and has surpassed larger institutional competitors in customer service and value. Although a pure Internet and telephone bank, SkandiaBanken's managers attribute their success to a business model that integrates simple IT infrastructure and web solutions, easy information access for customers and employees, and a company culture stressing transparency, personal responsibility, and action.

In practice

- Recognize that managing information depends upon people: how they use available information and systems, how they share their knowledge with others, and how motivated they are to use information to innovate and create value.

- Assess, develop, and improve the processes to manage information and knowledge. Remember that the technology itself, while essential for success, is not a corporate panacea.

- Find out more about information orientation from Professor Donald Marchand or IMD business school, or read about it in detail online (www.enterpriseiq.com) or in print in his book *Making the Invisible Visible*.

IDEA 7
Franchising

By selling a brand, a business plan, and expertise to regional business owners, corporations can increase profits and gain a global reach without significantly increasing risk.

The idea

The number and variety of franchises is large, and is a technique employed by companies ranging from McDonald's fast food outlets to the Hyatt luxury hotel chain. There are two key elements of any franchise – a franchiser and a franchisee. The franchiser sells its reputable brand and expertise to the franchisee, who then establishes and manages the business. The benefit for the franchiser is the ability to increase profit and become a nationally (or globally) known and trusted brand.

The benefit to the franchisee is, many believe, a reduced level of risk. It also provides increased ease, as the franchisee does not have to create a new business plan or develop an unknown brand.

Although the idea of franchising is an old one, it was invigorated in the late twentieth century, with an increased desire for decentralized business structures. By 1999, statistics indicated that there were 540,000 franchises in the USA, with a new one opening every 6.5 minutes of each business day.

Starbucks is a well-known franchise success story. Founded in 1971 with a single store in Seattle's Pike Place Market, it embraced franchising and, by 2006, had 8,000 locations in over 37 countries and profits nearing $3 billion.

In practice

- Ensure a consistent delivery of high-quality service and product across all franchises to gain a positive, stable, and trusted reputation among consumers.

- Setting up new franchises too close to existing ones can risk one of the operations being "cannibalized" and losing trade. Although this can be a positive business practice, it is important to consider the repercussions.

- Allow franchises to achieve a higher degree of independence, differentiating them from passive investors or conglomerates.

- Use expert, experienced lawyers or advisers to help – whether you are selling or buying a franchise. The key to success is to have the right business product or service, to be clear about the details, and to agree and work together.

IDEA 8
Eliminating waste (*muda*)

In the rush to focus on revenue, many businesses forget to consider the importance of business process and the effects of waste. Put another way, businesses that strive to remain streamlined and well-organized have a significant advantage over those that lack efficiency.

The idea

For decades, leading Japanese companies directed their cost management efforts toward *muda* (waste elimination). Western companies mirrored the success of this "Japanese Miracle" of the 1970s and 1980s. Concepts of just in time (JIT) and waste elimination meant that new terms, such as process analysis, process mapping, and re-engineering, became part of the business lexicon. The idea of process analysis is to think of business activities as a chain of events, perhaps from the beginning of the manufacturing process through to the end, and to break down the chain of activities into very discrete, yet identifiable tasks.

Following difficulties in the 1970s, senior managers at Harley-Davidson visited Honda's motorcycle facility at Marysville, Ohio. The difference between Honda's facility and Harley-Davidson's was dramatic in terms of layout, production flow, efficiency, and inventory management. The managers decided that Harley-Davidson needed to introduce a business-wide JIT manufacturing initiative called MAN (Materials As Needed). Production operations were brought together, reducing the amount of resources required for material handling. Harley-Davidson reduced both the amount of supplies received too early and the inventory produced too early. This also reduced the space required for manufacturing, which liberated additional space to increase production.

Caterpillar, a leading manufacturer of agricultural and construction machinery, had a similar experience. During the 1980s, Caterpillar's cost structure was significantly higher than its principal competitor – the Japanese firm Komatsu. Caterpillar concluded that Komatsu's "flow" process was more efficient than Caterpillar's method of moving parts and partially finished products through the production process. It undertook a significant plant rearrangement initiative called PWAF (Plant With a Future). The new flow process reduced the distances between operations, which improved material handling expenses, inventory levels, and cycle time to make each product. In some cases, cycle time was reduced by as much as 80 percent.

In practice

- Analyze your production process for inefficiency and wastage. Ask the people who run the processes how they could be improved. This applies to service businesses as well as manufacturing and process industries.

- Create a clear, workable plan for reducing areas of inefficiency and replacing them with streamlined operations.

- Decide what success will look like, how it will be measured, and when it will be assessed.

- Be cautious when introducing the new plan. Changes to any process can have unforeseen consequences – be aware of these possible problems and be ready to make adjustments to compensate for them.

IDEA 9
Customer bonding

As business competition becomes increasingly fierce, firms should not only focus on attracting new customers, they should also use rewards to retain existing clients and get more out of them, which will also attract more clients.

The idea

Many industries are characterized by the fight not only to attract customers but also to retain their continuing support once captured. An example of using information to enhance customer bonding and improve competitiveness is customer loyalty schemes. These schemes have long been a feature of marketing programs, with a recent example being Air Miles. There has been a large growth in the number and type of firms offering loyalty programs. These range from bookstores, such as WH Smith in the UK, which has a sophisticated database of millions of customers, through to credit card companies and telephone operators such as MCI in the USA, which pioneered the friends and family discount. For MCI, this single measure, undertaken with relatively modest advertising expenditure (5 percent of the market leader, AT&T), resulted in its market share growing by 4 percent despite fierce competition.

The inventiveness of loyalty programs is constantly surprising, revealing the brand values of the companies and the threat they pose to competitors. For example, Virgin Atlantic introduced an ingenious loyalty scheme for customer bonding, to reduce the time that it takes to get new customers. Virgin offers privileges to those involved in competitors' loyalty schemes, offering a free companion ticket to any British Airways frequent flyer who has accumulated 10,000 miles. This has the added advantage of reinforcing perceptions of the Virgin brand as being dynamic and flexible.

In practice

■ Create customer loyalty schemes to encourage repeat business and build up a positive brand image among your client base.

■ Focus on your competitors when creating a loyalty program. What are they offering, and what can you offer that is better and more enticing for the customer?

■ Be creative with loyalty programs and other methods of customer bonding. It is an area with many possibilities for innovation – take advantage of them.

■ Ask customer-facing employees how best to enhance customer loyalty.

IDEA 10
Psychographic profiling

To improve sales efficiency, customers can be divided into "groups" according to their personal needs and preferences; new customers can then be assessed and assigned to the appropriate group. This profiling combines psychological and demographic groupings – hence the term "psychographic." This enables the business to cater to customers' specific needs and preferences in a seamless and efficient way. This streamlining of customer knowledge allows companies to triumph in competitive and customer-focused markets.

The idea

"The Key to Happiness" was a self-diagnosis tool developed for Club Med customers. The business found that over 40 percent of customer dissatisfaction was directly linked to customers being recommended (or allowed to choose) the wrong type of location for their holiday. For example, a family would unwittingly choose a resort designed for single people, while a couple wanting to discover the local customs would mistakenly visit an empty island. Further studies revealed Club Med had five customer segments:

- *Tubes* who like to be comfortable and with their family.

- *Celebrators* who like to party.

- *Epicureans* who prefer a high level of comfort.

- *Cultivated guests* who like to discover the country – its culture, history, and charm.

- *Activists* who want to get in shape and enjoy sports.

"The Key to Happiness" was a self-service system designed to help customers. It worked by using questions to find out which of the five categories best suited the customer and which location would serve them best. As a result of this system, business grew both in the short term, as customers found what they wanted, and in the long term, as satisfied customers kept returning.

In practice

- Understand your clients. Who are they, and what do they want from your business? Customer feedback and surveys are useful sources of information to help you gather this information.

- Segment your market. Divide your customers into meaningful groups based on their personality, demands, and other relevant factors.

- Brainstorm ways your product can be tailored to best serve the interests of these individual groups.

- Assess each new client, to decide which of the "customer groups" they belong to – and then provide them with a more personalized service.

- Match all the elements of your offer – particularly pricing and extras – to precisely meet the needs of each client segment.

- Ensure that people in your business understand, value, and tailor their work to satisfy each type of customer.

- Be prepared to add new groups as required.

IDEA 11
Understanding demography

The world is changing fast, and one of the greatest changes in human history has taken place without many of us even noticing – the changes that result from demographic developments. Understanding these changes can provide a secure foundation as well as significant business opportunities.

The idea

The idea is simple: by understanding demography, future opportunities and threats will be revealed. One global business that understands the significance of demography is HSBC, "the world's local bank." Understanding the composition of populations, how they will change, and what each group in society will want is vital for long-term success if you are running a wide range of businesses – and especially financial services. Consider this HSBC email sent from its website (www.yourpointofview.com) in 2007:

> Tell us what you think. Do you agree with 57% of Indonesians who see retirement as a time for rest? Or, like 58% of Canadians, do you see it as the start of a new career? With more of us living longer these days, it's an issue that needs serious consideration. Especially given that, by 2050, 22% of the world's population may be living in retirement.

HSBC is developing a dynamic business in life, pensions, and investments, but that is just the start. Demography is behind many changes within HSBC. For example, HSBC has responded to migration from eastern Europe to the UK by recognizing that there is a demand among migrant workers for bank accounts and loans, even among people without a credit history in the UK, and immigrants also want to send remittances back to their families. This was not an isolated incident but a major new market segment, and HSBC developed and marketed (in several languages) a product that did just that.

The twentieth century saw unparalleled demographic change. Global population nearly quadrupled (from 1.6 billion in 1900 to 6.1 billion in 2000); there was the highest population growth rate (2 percent in 1969) and the shortest time for the global population to double, which it did between the administrations of US Presidents Kennedy and Clinton. This was combined with unprecedented declines in mortality and fertility, significant international migration, and increased urbanization – resulting in the emergence of mega-cities.

Clearly, demographic developments are changing the world around us. The fastest growing populations are in India, China, Pakistan, Nigeria, Indonesia, and Bangladesh. For example:

- Japan expects its population to decline by 50 percent by 2100, the result of a low birth rate and a very low level of immigration.

- Within ten years, Italy will have more than 1 million people aged over 90. Within Europe, Italy's population strength is in fast decline, together with Russia and Germany.

- The USA is the only major developed country with a population that is increasing, largely due to migration. By 2050, the USA will have a population of 400 million. Despite this, population growth is concentrated almost entirely in "developing" regions.

- Demographic developments are changing family composition

in the developing world, with the result that the influence of women is increasing.

■ Populations will be older than ever before, with profound implications for welfare policies, pensions, taxation, employment, and spending throughout the affected economies of the developed world.

■ Urbanization is widespread and rising. In 2006, for the first time in human history, global urban population exceeded global rural population. This movement to cities, like much demographic change, will profoundly alter behavior and expectations.

In practice

Understand how demography might be affecting your key markets. What are the trends? Where are the opportunities and threats? Who are your customers now and who will they be in the future?

IDEA 12
Mass customization

Large-scale information gathering and storing enables the provision of a high-quality, personalized service for each client. By adding value to your product, you can shut out competitors and ensure repeat business.

The idea

By applying information technology effectively, and training all of its employees to use information, the Ritz-Carlton hotel chain has, over the last 15 years, developed into one of the most successful luxury hotel chains in the world, providing customers with a highly personalized service. The Ritz-Carlton strategy was quite simple: to differentiate itself from its competitors by offering distinctive service and customer value at a competitive price.

What was uncommon, however, was the emphasis on several key principles, which were underpinned by a blend of strong leadership and the successful management and application of technology. These principles included:

- A vision of an efficient, personalized service. It was important to ensure employees were committed to providing a quality service. IT systems were standardized throughout the business, and an organizational culture was developed that emphasized the need to capture and disseminate useful information about each individual customer.

■ The desire to ensure hotels operated error-free and to retain customers through a precision marketing strategy. To achieve this, Ritz-Carlton spent years accumulating in-depth knowledge about its work processes, then combined technology with individual skills and innovation, which has enabled Ritz-Carlton to track individual customer preferences.

For instance, employees observe guests, record their preferences, and store the data on a company-wide information network. This enables other employees to reuse the information and provide the most personalized service available, leveraging their contact with the customer to shut out competitors. When customers check in they receive the room and location they prefer, and throughout their stay Ritz-Carlton supervisors scrutinize relevant details for each customer so that they can personalize service, providing extra pillows, favorite beverages, preferred newspapers, and so forth.

The Ritz-Carlton approach is a great example of the power of mass customization – the ability to deliver rapidly, efficiently, and profitably a range of products and services satisfying each individual customer.

In practice

■ Utilize employees at every level within your company, as well as the benefits of technology, to listen to your market at a uniquely advanced level.

■ Store information on clients in an easily accessible way, to ensure that a distinguished level of personalized quality is provided.

- Swiftly reorganize people, information, and processes when necessary in order to deliver the benefits of a highly customized and attentive service.

IDEA 13
Leading "top-down" innovation

Direct action should be taken by senior management to harness the knowledge and ideas of employees to ensure consistent and high-quality innovation.

The idea

The word "innovation" conjures up the image of a process that is spontaneous, unpredictable, and unmanageable. The innovation literature abounds with stories of serendipitous discoveries and independent-minded champions doggedly pursuing an idea until they hit the jackpot. Often – as the stories stress – inventors worked in secret against the will of management. The archetypes of such innovators are Art Fry and Spence Silver, the 3M chemists who turned a poorly sticking adhesive into a billion-dollar blockbuster: Post-It notes. In these cases, innovation proceeded in a bottom-up fashion, with ideas and the drive to see them through originating in labs or marketing outposts – not from the top of the organization. However, to ensure consistent and high quality innovation, the role of management is vital.

Senior management should take significant and direct action, using information and knowledge. The commercial development of the credit card is an example. In 1958, a research group at the Bank of America called the Customer Services Research Department, with the remit to develop potential new products, created the first credit card. This development was augmented later by seven bankers at Citibank who added further key features, including merchant discounts, credit limits, and terms and conditions.

This development did not occur in response to a market need: it emerged because people within the banking business used their knowledge and information. This included market-sensing abilities, understanding of customers, information and forecasts about economic and social trends, experience with similar product ideas (such as installment loans), and knowledge about new developments in technology. A period of major innovation within the financial services industry followed, including ATM machines and the growth of internet banking.

This type of innovation is markedly different from bottom-up innovation:

- Senior management support was essential: they set up the unit, helped to develop its features, and gave it the support needed to take root and grow.

- The senior management role was significant *early on* in the process, creating the right conditions and providing support and momentum.

- Information was at the heart of this top-down innovation. Harnessing information and tacit knowledge is an essential part of ensuring that the innovation process starts, continues, and delivers success.

In practice

- Encourage senior management to become directly involved in the innovation process.

- Use the market-sensing abilities, knowledge, and experience of team members to evaluate innovative ideas.

- Create a "culture of innovation" within your organization by giving employees a forum to discuss and evaluate their ideas, and rewarding innovation.

IDEA 14
Social networking and transmitting company values

Regular meetings of key employees from different areas of the company will increase learning, improve strategy, remove boundaries, and increase group productivity. The improved "transparency" that results will make it easier to identify crucial areas of strength and weakness.

The idea

General Electric's employees started to listen more attentively to CEO Jack Welch's simple speeches on the company's values following the company's unprecedented restructuring during the early 1980s, which included divestments in over 200 GE companies and massive layoffs of around 135,000 people. The resulting company was considerably less bureaucratic, underlying the CEO's message of simplicity, candor, and transparent learning across boundaries.

To underline this, Jack Welch personally started a series of "work-outs" or "town meetings" – which were simply gatherings of key managers across functional and geographic boundaries – where difficult issues were discussed openly and candid learning was fostered around the CEO's leadership. As a result, there were fewer and fewer places to hide in GE's global managerial ranks throughout the 1980s.

Individuals who survived their CEO's grinding communications rituals were capable of passing on to others the simple message of simplicity, candor, and transparent learning across boundaries. Most of Welch's social networking took place at GE's corporate university at Crotonville, where he reputedly spent over 50 percent of his time constantly coaching, and learning from others.

In practice

- Reduce bureaucracy to increase the transparency and openness of your organization.

- Identify key employees across the business, and organize regular meetings to share ideas, report problems, and devise strategy. Use these meetings to assess workers: who is best at innovation and identifying problems, and who is weakest?

- Create a robust social network within your organization that can be used to transmit information and implement ideas promptly. This may involve bringing representatives from a wide range of "departments" to meetings. For example, rather than holding separate meetings for IT employees and marketing employees, allow them to discuss ideas together. This will give them a clearer idea of the challenges faced by the company as a whole.

- Hold regular meetings of global managers, to ensure they are unified behind the initiative and understand how it should be implemented. Also, encourage global managers to meet with members of their business unit to inform them of the company initiative.

- Provide incentives to managers to win their team members over – for example, by giving them performance-based rewards for their business unit's success in implementing specific initiatives.

IDEA 15
Achieving breakthrough growth

Established businesses often struggle to achieve industry-leading growth rates because their sector is mature or highly competitive, or because they become stuck in the rut of incrementalism. Firms become convinced that they need to compete in the same way as their rivals: minimizing risk, maximizing resources, and making acceptable returns. There is another way: fundamentally reconceive what drives your profits, build a better business model, and achieve breakthrough growth.

The idea

Research by business school professors Rita Gunther McGrath and Ian C. MacMillan highlights how companies in a range of industries achieve exceptional growth (see *Marketbusters: 40 Strategic Moves That Drive Exceptional Business Growth*, published by Harvard Business School Press). The key is to revise your business, taking a new, different, and radical approach from that of your competitors and finding better ways to drive profits. It is essential to be flexible and creative, and to understand what customers value.

Cemex transformed its small commodity business in Monterey, Mexico, into one of the largest cement companies in the world through a radical reassessment of what would drive profits. It has outperformed its international rivals, Holcim and Lafarge, in share price, operating margins, and return on assets. Cemex moved from selling concrete as a product by the yard, to selling timely delivery of a commodity. Delivery was what mattered to customers: getting the right amount, in the right place at the right time, without workers waiting or the concrete spoiling. Using methods employed by Federal Express and ambulance crews, Cemex developed digital technology to manage the location and dispatch of its trucks. Now, Cemex uses GPS technology to guarantee delivery of ready-mix cement within a 20-minute window.

In practice

For Cemex, success was based on a cultural change across the business. This required a proactive approach to meeting commitments, developing new ways of serving customers, and ensuring efficient operations. Using the following techniques can achieve breakthrough growth:

- *Transform the customer's experience* and find new ways to meet their needs – e.g. Microsoft developed Office software, and whatever you think of their business it's definitely got the edge over typewriting!

- *Transform the product or service offered to customers* so it reflects what they value. One approach is to compare your offer with competitors' by sorting product attributes into three categories: basic, differentiated, and exceptional. Then consider how to develop new advantages and strengthen existing ones to make your product exceptional.

- *Change your performance metrics* so you can monitor and improve your customer offer.

- *Redefine your business*, possibly by altering the fundamental unit that customers are charged for, or by revising key metrics used to measure how well you are selling. For example, some lawyers departed from the traditional method of selling their time to selling services on a "no win, no fee" basis.

- *Capitalize on changes in your sector.* For example, Amazon.com recognized the potential for the internet to redefine retailing. Also, HSBC bank was the first to recognize that immigrants in the UK had specific banking needs (e.g. to repatriate funds from overseas) and circumstances (no banking history in the UK), and offered products tailored to suit this market.

IDEA 16
Deep-dive prototyping

A deep-dive process is a focused, team approach to developing solutions to specific problems or challenges. It is intended to harness the ideas of everyone in a team in a creative, stimulating, focused, energetic, fun, and useful way.

The idea

A deep dive is a combination of brainstorming and prototyping (where an initial potential solution is explored and developed). This is an approach that anyone leading a change initiative can use to identify actions that can move a business forward. A deep dive can be completed in an hour, a day, or a week.

The main stages in the deep-dive process are:

- Building a varied team.

- Defining the design challenge.

- Visiting experts.

- Sharing ideas.

- Brainstorming and voting.

- Developing a fast prototype.

- Testing and refining the prototype.

- Focusing on the prototype and producing a final solution.

In practice

IDEO, a prominent US design company, believes that there are several stages in deep-dive prototyping (for further information see *The Art of Innovation: Lessons in creativity from IDEO, America's leading design firm* by Tom Kelley and Jonathan Littman).

- Understand your market, customers, technology, and perceived constraints.

- Observe people in real life situations.

- Synthesize and organize the key themes from the first two phases.

- Visualize: this often involves intensive brainstorming and discussion. Imagine new concepts and ideas around the main themes of the design.

- Prototyping is next, and this involves building ideas and physical brainstorming.

- Refine and streamline your ideas. Again, brainstorm ways to improve the prototype and overcome obstacles, and narrow and focus your concepts. Evaluate and prioritize your ideas, and decide how they will be implemented.

Other valuable aspects of creative problem solving that may be applied when time is tight include:

- trying first (and asking for forgiveness later)
- test marketing

- ensuring that teams are as varied and diverse as possible

- seeking external input

- reducing, and virtually eliminating, hierarchy

- involving people, generating a sense of play, and working without boundaries

- being flexible about working arrangements

- accepting that it is all right to try and fail

- imposing a deadline, while allowing people the time to be creative.

IDEA 17
Market testing

The finest place to develop a profitable business, and the best way of building success, is often when you are already operating a business. Lessons can be taken directly from the market and your customers to give you an instant guide on what is working – and what isn't.

The idea

Julian Metcalfe and Sinclair Beecham founded the successful Pret A Manger chain of sandwich shops 20 years ago. It has gained substantial profits, been credited with "reinventing the sandwich," and become familiar in the UK, New York, and Hong Kong.

Yet their business did not start out as a sandwich shop; the original store was an off-licence (liquor store) in Fulham, London, called "Hair of the Dog." However, they soon realized this was not a winning formula. Although takings were high, the profit margin was not – Sinclair Beecham stated, "We decided there was more scope in low-priced, high-margin foods like sandwiches." By listening to clients and having a bold readiness to drastically alter the customer offering when necessary, they became successful.

This was a lesson they learnt firsthand while actively doing business in the market. Because any marketplace will always have a degree of unpredictability, the best way to learn the formula for a high-profit business is by "learning as you go."

This is not a lesson that Sinclair Beecham has forgotten. Preparing to launch the Hoxton in late 2006, an innovative "budget luxury" hotel in central London, he commented, "The Hoxton is an experiment. We'll see if it works. There'll be things that we need to change, and we'll listen to our customers if we need to do so."

In practice

- When starting a new business, do not expect to achieve a flawless formula instantly. No matter how much abstract preparation is done beforehand, there will always be lessons that can only be learnt on the "shop floor."

- Do not be discouraged when problems are encountered. View them not as obstacles or failures but as invaluable opportunities for learning. Analyze why they occurred, their significance, and their impact.

- Be prepared to make drastic changes to your business. Although it can be tempting to hold onto a particular formula, it may have to be altered, or in extreme cases discarded, for a more profitable alternative.

- Combine abstract learning with hands-on experience. The two concepts do not have to be mutually exclusive.

IDEA 18
Empowering your customers

The importance of providing information to the client should not be underestimated. Information encourages customers to buy and to get the maximum out of the service being provided. Conversely, businesses should be eager to accept information from the consumer in the form of customer satisfaction and feedback surveys.

The idea

From 1989 to 1991, Ryder – the largest truck-leasing business in the world – suffered a steady decline in its business and slipped to second place in its core US market. To address this problem, Ryder recognized the need to use information more effectively to serve customers. Its approach highlighted three key influences affecting current and potential customers:

1. *The need to help customers buy*: for example, by producing a brochure explicitly explaining why they should buy Ryder's insurance, as well as providing another brochure offering other supplies and accessories. Ryder recognized that customers would want to compare products with competitors, so it produced a truck comparison chart, highlighting its competitiveness and reassuring potential customers.

2. *The need to help customers use the service*: Ryder provided a free guide to moving to every customer and potential customer, published in Spanish and English.

3. *The need to help customers to continuously adapt their usage:* as well as ensuring that each outlet was well ordered, displaying a strong sense of corporate identity and commitment to customer service, Ryder ensured that there were additional products and services available at its outlets. These included information about the advantages of using Ryder's towing equipment and details of longer-term discount rates.

The benefit of these measures to customers was closely monitored with a customer satisfaction survey, prominently placed in each truck cab. Apart from checking customer satisfaction, they highlighted Ryder's renewed commitment to service, enhancing future sales prospects. This approach contributed to Ryder's ability to turn around its business.

In practice

- Ensure that existing and potential customers have easily available information about the various services and benefits your company offers.

- Collect feedback from clients to ensure their satisfaction and to present an image of your company as customer focused.

- Enable customers to use your product – provide them with instructional information, ideas, online guides, people to talk with – anything that will empower the customer and help them adapt your product to their needs.

IDEA 19
Cannibalizing

Instead of allowing other companies to eat into your market, consider bringing in new products to compete with your existing ones. This may sound like suicide, but handled expertly it allows you to remain on the cutting edge and ahead of the competition.

The idea

When there is a limited market for a particular product or service, any new competitors may consume the market. A possible response to counter this is cannibalization – bringing in new products to compete with your existing offering. This is a tactic used by a surprisingly large number of businesses, from the café franchise Starbucks to the technology manufacturer Intel.

Starbucks' well-known tendency to open branches within minutes of each other represents a fierce desire to keep competition at bay. Even though these branches will be competing with each other for a limited number of clients, Starbucks has recognized that this is preferable to competing with other potential market leaders, such as Costa Coffee and Caffé Nero.

Manufacturers of computer hardware and software, such as Apple, Intel, and Microsoft, are other well-known examples of cannibalization. By regularly bringing out upgraded versions of their products (i.e. faster computers or more virus-resistant software) they not only remain at the cutting edge of the industry, they also persuade customers to purchase new products, and allow less room for competitors to encroach into their market. This works well in fickle markets with limited loyalty (for example, Starbucks may feel that people wanting a coffee may be prepared to get it from anywhere). It also works when people want, for whatever reason, to keep up to date – for example, with the latest technological developments.

In practice

- Judge market conditions in order to decide precisely when to cannibalize a particular product. Developing a product often takes time and money – if the existing product is highly profitable and not at risk from competitors, postpone the introduction of a new offering to a time when it is necessary or desirable.

- Cannibalize when it is anticipated that a competitor will introduce a potentially popular new product.

- When sales are stagnating, cannibalizing your older products with more cutting-edge offerings can radically stimulate overall sales.

- Do not be afraid of competing with yourself. Although it may seem daunting at first to risk cutting off the market for your older products, it should be recognized as a positive way to handle the cut-throat, dynamic nature of modern business. Also it will force you to innovate and overcome complacency.

IDEA 20
Increasing competitiveness

Competition requires a large amount of effort and business acumen: most businesses will, at some time, have to face circumstances that are exceptionally challenging and strenuous. There are a number of tactics and techniques that can help guide an organization through troubled times.

The idea

Many organizations are familiar with the challenge of maintaining productivity and profitability when the industry is threatened – whether that threat comes from global unrest, supplier shortages, or simply the presence of increasingly threatening competitors.

Among notorious examples of companies that have been unable to cope with such challenges, the case of Air France is a refreshing success story. The example of Air France is all the more impressive given the significant, continuing pressures faced by the airline industry. In common with other established carriers in Europe and North America, it found traditional markets threatened by increasing security concerns, the downturn in the airline industry, and the rise of low-cost carriers. To remain competitive, Air France paid special attention to four techniques:

- *Reacting rapidly:* Air France's main decisions following the 9/11 crisis were taken on September 18, 2001; they were later adjusted and developed, but the new strategy was developed and implemented quickly.

- *Acting collectively:* the board meets to react quickly, considering how best to respond to events and how to coordinate its response.

- *Constantly looking at all competitors:* this keeps the business lean and focused on what matters. In France, there has been an established lower-cost competitor since 1981 – the TGV high-speed train. This has meant that many of the disciplines needed for competing with low-cost operators have been developed over many years.

- *Using all available resources:* competing has meant employing all of the assets and advantages that a big industrial carrier has in order to counter low-cost operators – including brand, market position, and operational strengths. Often a competitor's strategy is to build market share with temporary low prices and then to raise them. An active and patient approach can help to reduce or remove the threat of competitors.

In practice

- Actively communicate your brand values – what it is that makes your organization and product special and preferable.

- Benchmark your business against other organizations.

- Meet with customers and understand their perceptions and needs.

- Understand, strengthen, and preserve the causes of success in the business.

- Find out why customers prefer you to your competitors.

- Review competitors' strengths and weaknesses regularly. Develop an action plan that, over time, will minimize these strengths and exploit weaknesses.

- Develop and refine products and the tactics used to sell, taking into account your understanding of the competition.

IDEA 21
Clustering

By setting up in "industry centers" where similar businesses are clustered together, firms gain instant access to a large and varied range of benefits.

The idea

The idea of clustering seems counter-intuitive. It suggests that firms should pay high real estate prices to be positioned close to their competitors. Although there are many businesses that prefer cheaper real estate farther from the threat of competitors, clustering is surprisingly common in many industries. From the shops of Oxford Street in London to the technology companies of Silicon Valley, clustering has a far-reaching appeal.

The benefits of clustering are particularly relevant to new businesses. It affords easy access to an already established network of customers, suppliers, and information. It can also help build reputation – it encourages customers to associate your organization with the other respected and long-established businesses in the area.

Clustering is also a blessing for the firm in a highly competitive industry, like selling cars. While it remains easier for customers to choose your rival over you when it is positioned next-door, a company with a truly superior, competitive offering has little to fear from this.

One of the most famous examples of clustering is the entertainment industry of Hollywood, where freelancers and small firms prospered by locating near the studios. Further north there is the example of Silicon Valley – a cluster of technology companies benefiting from the pool of talent in nearby universities.

Although clustering raises a number of challenges for any business to overcome, an innovative, efficient, and dynamic company will be able to turn these challenges into unrivaled advantages.

In practice

- There are often a number of industry centers for a particular product; use careful research to decide which one best suits your business.

- Ensure your customer offering is truly competitive – the direct contrast with rival companies provided by clustering will only benefit companies with genuinely superior products.

- Highlight where you are and emphasize how your products are superior.

- Take advantage of the increased access to cutting-edge industry information – this can range from regional publications to "neighborhood gossip."

- Remember that clustering is not suitable for all companies – consider your overall business plan and the nature of your business before deciding where to locate.

IDEA 22
Highlighting unique selling points (USPs)

Products should have at least one USP: a factor that differentiates and elevates them above their competitors.

The idea

The idea of a "unique selling point" seems to underpin the very nature of competition. It suggests that every product should have an effective, direct, and easily summarized "selling point" that appeals to the customer and is not shared by competitors. Yet surprisingly few businesses have actually employed this idea, content merely to meet the industry standard without surpassing it, relying solely on market momentum for profitability. This approach was rejected by Tesco – the UK's largest retail chain – which decided instead to go the extra mile for market superiority. It took the decision to remain open 24 hours a day, becoming the first UK supermarket to do so. Tesco also introduced a number of other USPs – including the promise to open checkouts for customers if there was more than one person in front, and providing a complimentary bag-packing service (a service that is still a rare concept in the UK).

As well as "practical" USPs there are "emotional" USPs. While they may not seem to provide a practical advantage to the customer, they enable businesses to differentiate themselves and their products by using marketing to trigger emotional reactions in prospective clients. These reactions include the desire for status or a feeling of success. Luxury car manufacturer Mercedes-Benz is a prime example. Although its cars feature many practical advantages, it is arguable that its mainstream success is due to people with limited knowledge of cars and a desire to project a certain image of themselves in society.

Constant striving for USPs is what drives an industry forward, prevents stagnation, and benefits both consumers and the profits of successfully differentiated organizations.

In practice

- Recognize that your USP may well have to be dynamic and quickly changing. If it is successful, it is likely that competitors will begin to mimic it. Innovate to find new USPs and remain ahead of the competition.

- Find out what it is that your customers value most, currently lack, and will pay for – and develop this as your USP. This may be the product's benefits to them, its price, or the service they receive.

- Offer the highest quality: this can ensure your product gains both a practical USP and an emotional, status-oriented USP.

- Offer the widest choice – this can involve specializing and segmenting your market.

IDEA 23
The experience curve

Increases in production allow workers to become more experienced – and firms with experienced workers are able to reduce their costs and increase their revenues.

The idea

In the mid-1960s, Boston Consulting Group (BCG) noticed that a manufacturer of semiconductors was able to cut unit production costs by 25 percent every time it doubled its production level. It was concluded this was because the workers gained valuable experience, which allowed them to be become more efficient.

A slight variation of the traditional "economies of scale" principle, the idea's emphasis on employee experience has a range of broad, strategic implications that should be taken into consideration when deciding which workers to hire and how much to produce.

However, the effects of the experience curve are not universal to all companies and industries. Although it is generally estimated that a cost reduction of 20–30 percent will occur when experience doubles, there are many firms that deviate from these figures, with some only gaining a cost reduction of 5 percent. This is thought to be because different production processes provide different opportunities for gaining experience. It is also not feasible for many firms to drastically increase their production levels when there is a fixed demand for a product or when the production process is highly time-consuming and complex. It should also be noted that some firms simply do not have the resources to increase their production.

Nevertheless, the experience curve has valuable lessons for every company, even those that cannot actually increase production. Experience can be gained secondhand, through books, videos, and "mentoring" by individuals who are already experienced. Alternatively, firms can hire workers that are already experienced veterans of their industry (although it is usually necessary to pay higher salaries to such workers). Also, businesses that are currently inexperienced can use innovation to bring out new products, change market preferences, and render a competitor's experience obsolete.

In practice

- Encourage employees to view their job as an active learning experience.

- Recognize when it is not appropriate to increase your production – if your demand is fixed, then increased output will lead to wastage.

- Avoid high employee turnover by finding out why people leave.

- Provide opportunities for workers to gain secondhand experience (for example, through reading and teaching) as well as firsthand experience in the production process.

IDEA 24
The employee–customer–profit chain

Sears provides one of the best examples of employee practices connecting directly with organizational performance. The employee–customer–profit chain (a variation on the service profit chain) makes explicit the links between cause and effect. By enabling employees to see the implications of their actions, it can change the way people think and the results they achieve.

The idea

Traditionally, managers focus on results. However, this data is historical. What is really required for market leadership is an emphasis on managing value drivers (the aspects of the business that make the greatest difference and provide most benefit to customers). Of these value drivers, employee retention, employee satisfaction, and employee productivity significantly affect customer satisfaction, revenue growth, and profitability. This is highlighted below in the service profit chain.

In the early 1990s, senior executives at US-based retailer Sears realized that future performance was not going to improve simply by developing a different strategy or adjusting marketing plans. Following significant losses, executives focused on three issues:

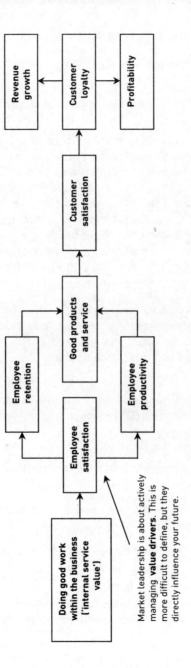

Market leadership is about actively managing **value drivers**. This is more difficult to define, but they directly influence your future.

Diagram: the service profit chain (SPC)

- how employees felt about working at Sears

- how employee behavior affected customers' shopping experience

- how customers' shopping experience affected profits.

Sears asked 10 percent of its workforce how much profit they thought was made for each dollar of sales. The average answer was 46 cents, whereas in reality it was *1 cent*. This highlighted the need for employees, especially those at the front line, to better understand the issues determining profitability. Sears' approach was to develop the employee–customer–profit model (ECPM), making explicit the chain of cause and effect. Because employees were better able to see the implications of their actions, it changed the way they thought and acted. This, in turn, was reflected in bottom-line performance.

The Sears approach to creating an ECPM (which is a specific version of the service profit chain) started by devising a set of measures based on objectives in three areas: making Sears a compelling place to work, a compelling place to shop, and a compelling place to invest.

For the top 200 managers at Sears, incentives are based on total performance indicators (TPI) – which include non-financial and financial measures.

- one-third on employee measures – attitude about the job and company

- one-third on customer measures – customer impression and retention

- one-third on financial measures – return on assets, operating margin, and revenue growth.

As a result of the employee–customer–profit chain, managers at Sears are recruited, promoted, and appraised on the basis of 12 criteria:

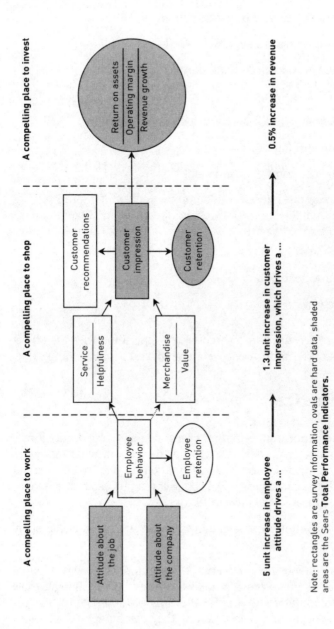

A compelling place to work

Attitude about the job

Attitude about the company

Employee behavior

Employee retention

A compelling place to shop

Service / Helpfulness

Merchandise / Value

Customer recommendations

Customer impression

Customer retention

A compelling place to invest

Return on assets
Operating margin
Revenue growth

5 unit increase in employee attitude drives a ...

→ 1.3 unit increase in customer impression, which drives a ...

→ 0.5% increase in revenue

Note: rectangles are survey information, ovals are hard data, shaded areas are the Sears **Total Performance Indicators.**

Diagram: the employee–customer–profit chain

- customer service orientation

- initiative and sense of urgency

- business knowledge and literacy

- problem solving

- developing associates and valuing their ideas

- teamworking skills

- two-way communication skills

- valuing diversity

- empowerment skills

- interpersonal skills

- change leadership

- integrity.

These are grouped into three areas – the three Ps: passion for the customer, performance leadership, and people adding value.

In practice

- Find opportunities for managers and marketing professionals to share customer data. HR has data about what motivates and engages people, whilst marketing has insights about external customers' needs. Develop a process that manages the causal links between factors.

- Blend intuition and common sense with sound statistical analysis.

- Understand the elements of workforce success – what makes employees productive, effective, and willing to use their initiative to achieve the organization's goals. Awareness of these issues and how they can be applied provides

HR with another essential role in ensuring the firm's commercial success.

- Make sure that measures are not over-complicated or excessively elaborate, when what is needed is a practical, robust, and informed approach.

IDEA 25
Measuring employees' performance

Recent research suggests that the average company spends 40 percent of its revenues on people-related expenses (human capital costs), and 92 percent of financial directors think human capital has a "huge" impact on customer satisfaction and profitability. However, only 16 percent of companies have any real idea of the return on human capital investments. The solution is to measure the direct return on your investments in people.

The idea

Given the sums invested in human capital activities – notably training and development – and the clear link between investment in employees and effectiveness, the need for systems to measure performance is vital. According to General Electric's former CEO, Jack Welch: "The three most important things you need to measure in a business are customer satisfaction, employee satisfaction and cash flow." Although Welch later changed the last item to shareholder value, the importance of the other two – and their connection – remains strong.

Executives typically encounter one or more problems with performance measurement.

- Too many measures obscure the most significant issues and divert attention from other issues.

- Measures are disconnected, unrelated to the firm's strategy and business priorities.

- Results are emphasized without necessarily providing an adequate explanation of how they were achieved.

- Rewards are not in line with measures of performance; consequently, the desired behaviors are not encouraged.

- Measurement is divisive, failing to support team-based working and collaboration.

- Short-termism is encouraged, as measurement leads to an intense focus on improving the next quarter's results.

Watson and Wyatt's *Human Capital Index* highlights the impact of people management practices, with five issues directly affecting profits:

1. Total rewards and accountability.

2. Collegial, flexible working place.

3. Recruitment and retention.

4. Open and honest communications.

5. Focused HR service technologies.

One approach to measuring the link between investments in people and performance is provided by B&Q's "Employee Engagement Programme." This prioritizes employee engagement and customer loyalty. Every manager has a regular, one-page report summarizing their performance in two areas: *managing human capital* and *managing traditional finance measures*.

As a result, employee turnover reduced from 35 percent to 28 percent (each percentage point of attrition costs at least £1 million), and profits increased, with turnover per employee rising from £87,000 in 1998 to £106,000 in 2002. The role of the finance team is central to the success of the process: designing, funding, and managing the program. Other features of the program include close liaison between HR and retail operations, objective measurements directly focusing actions on enhancing performance, and staff commitment to the program.

In practice

- Recognize that including "people" measures in an overall corporate scorecard raises the profile of human capital and ensures management focus. There is a connection between strong people practices, increased customer satisfaction, and financial results.

- Choosing the right HR measures means finding the link between motivating staff and achieving vital business outcomes – including issues as diverse as product innovation, safety, and customer satisfaction.

- Ensure top-level commitment to finding out and using this information.

- Provide active support for front-line managers.

- Recognize the importance and impact of discretionary behavior.

IDEA 26
Brand spaces

Developing stylish areas that are decorated and designed to appeal to your target market, even if they do not sell your core products, will reinforce your image and help customers appreciate the distinctiveness of your products and brand.

The idea

One of the trendiest new ideas in marketing, brand spaces advocates creating stylish spaces – perhaps a bar, art gallery, lounge, or exhibition hall – that may not be directly related to your main product but where individuals are immersed in your brand image. Practiced by leading companies such as Apple, ING Direct, Kodak, Google, and Nokia, there has been a dramatic increase in the number and quality of brand spaces.

French car manufacturer Renault uses brand spaces with a high level of commitment and panache, running four brand spaces in Buenos Aires, Bogota, Mexico City, and Paris. Its latest project, the Terrasse Renault in Mexico City, is impressively designed, and centers on "a bar with wooden latticing, through which visitors can glimpse the Renault zone, where car prototypes are exhibited." Occupying prime real estate in global cities and offering gourmet cuisine, art galleries, and seamlessly blended marketing, the Renault brand spaces are characteristic of the concept. Renault describes its brand spaces as "hosting artistic, cultural and sporting events in keeping with the brand's universe to reinforce Renault's energy and identity as a visionary, warm and innovative brand."

The innovative design of brand spaces includes Nokia's "silence booths" for people seeking temporary quiet and calm at music festivals; Coca-Cola's "Red Lounges" designed to provide multimedia experiences to teenagers in malls in Illinois and Los Angeles, and Microsoft's Xbox 360 Lounge in Tokyo incorporating VIP rooms, multimedia opportunities, and even Xbox-themed mixed drinks.

With an increase in lifestyle brands, brand spaces can reinforce your organization as part of an idealized culture and aesthetic that is sculpted to the tastes of your target demographic. Brand spaces help sell directly and indirectly. They also build the value of your business by generating understanding of – and affinity for – your brand.

In practice

- Consider where your target demographic market would choose to go to enjoy their free time and use your brand space to create an idealized version of it.

- Recognize the variety of options you have when creating a brand space; focus on individuality.

- Remember that the aesthetic and physical design of the brand space is usually vital.

- Choose which specific aspects of your company's service and image will be portrayed in the space.

- Provide a range of activities for visitors to enjoy.

- Decide what the emphasis of your brand space will be – for example, convenience, culture, excitement, or relaxation.

- Choose your location carefully – whether you choose an airport, shopping center, music festival, or simply a city street to be home to your brand space, is the first step to ensuring the project is a success.

IDEA 27
Being spaces

Creating places where people want to be – whether to socialize, relax, or simply carry out everyday activities such as reading or working – can become a profitable product.

The idea

At first glance, this concept appears similar to "brand spaces." However, there is a crucial difference: "being spaces" make the idea of a desirable social setting the chief selling point and core product – a fundamental aspect of the business.

Being spaces are particularly popular in cities where cramped apartments, claustrophobic offices, and sometimes unsafe public areas prompt people to seek a more relaxing change of scene. Trend Watching, an organization documenting consumer trends, described the concept of being spaces as "... urban dwellers trading their lonely, cramped living rooms for the real-life buzz of commercial living-room-like settings, where catering and entertainment aren't just the main attraction, but are there to facilitate small office/living room activities like watching a movie, reading a book, meeting friends and colleagues, or doing your admin."

While many successful businesses, such as coffee house franchise Starbucks and book retailers Borders, blend the idea of a being space with other products, there is an increasing number of businesses devoted to providing customers with nothing other than simply a place to be. Paragraph NY is one such company. With monthly memberships from $100, it provides a 2,500 square foot loft space near Union Square divided into a writing room and a lounge area. Members can work in library-style cubicles or relax and socialize with other members – a modern home from home.

In practice

- Design the space carefully and functionally – emphasize style and comfort, and use soft furnishings and room dividers to absorb sound, ensuring your being space remains convivial and relaxed.

- Provide opportunities both for socializing and relative privacy within the space.

- Consider raising revenue by selling advertising in the being space. While you should not allow advertising to compromise the aesthetic feeling, sophisticated, cutting-edge, and carefully placed adverts can enhance customers' perceptions and be useful.

- Even if you do not wish to have a being space as your primary business venture you can incorporate some of the principles into your business to entice potential customers.

IDEA 28
Increasing accessibility

By offering flexible opening hours, businesses can differentiate themselves and attract customers with varying lifestyles.

The idea

As society changes, lifestyles have developed and diversified. An increasing demand for convenience and freedom has overtaken the market in recent years, providing competitive advantage for corporations that cater to the demands of the 24-hour consumer.

By remaining open for business 24 hours a day, there is the obvious potential of increased trade. Slightly less obvious is the advantage of building a perception among your customers of being different, customer-oriented, and convenient. It is also an opportunity to attract customers that may not have used your store, as you may be the only business open. These new clients may then continue visiting your business even when other competitors are open.

UK retail giant Tesco employed this strategy with impressive results. The only UK supermarket to remain open 24 hours a day, it broke from its close rivalry with other chain stores to gain a convincing lead within the market.

This technique has also been employed by a range of other companies courting customers with disposable income and difficult schedules – certain London estate agents (realtors) offer a late-night service for busy individuals. Don't be put off by a lack of a "standard schedule" for your customer – use it as an opportunity to prosper in the "24-hour society" by becoming a 24-hour business.

In practice

- If your organization is unready or unsuited for the move towards all-day trading, it is possible to choose only select areas of your business (such as customer service) that will remain open 24 hours a day.

- Using a skeleton staff and minimizing operations can cut costs during times you are open but not conducting much trade – such as late at night or early in the morning.

- Ensure a positive experience for customers, even at the times when using a skeleton staff. The quality of their experience will decide whether they return in future.

- Be flexible – for example, many businesses comply with UK Sunday trading laws by opening early for browsing but not allowing any actual purchases until the legally permitted time.

- Offering 24-hour opening can be challenging for smaller firms, but it is possible to accommodate complex customer schedules by simply offering flexible opening hours.

IDEA 29
Partnering

With commercial partnerships, firms can pool resources and achieve complex goals that might otherwise have been out of their individual reach.

The idea

By organizing a corporate partnership it is possible to use your competitor's resources – such as transport networks, physical structures, raw materials, knowledge, and customer reputation – to realize the full potential of an ambitious idea that would otherwise rely on your acquiring an unfeasibly large number of new resources. Such deals can be negotiated by either giving partners a share of profits, or by arranging a mutual relationship where they are allowed to use your resources in return.

Oneworld Alliance – a partnership between eight major airlines (British Airways, Cathay Pacific, Aer Lingus, Finn Air, Iberia, LAN, Qantas, and American Airlines) – utilizes corporate partnerships to offer a service they could not provide separately. The service is an inclusive, low-cost round-the-world fare where customers pay a one-off fee to travel to a wide range of global destinations. Because customers can travel on any airline within the Oneworld Alliance, the scheme offers the customer the opportunity to travel to over 600 destinations in 135 countries. This highly successful service is staying true to its dynamic image, with plans to incorporate three new partners (Japan Airlines, Malév, and Royal Jordanian). It also provides a helpful way to comply with the restrictive rules in the aviation industry governing ownership of airlines, in a way that benefits customers.

In practice

- Avoid any unethical or illegal business practices that can be associated with corporate partnerships, such as price fixing.

- Assess, in depth, the specific terms and implications of the partnership agreement. Will your partner get more out of it than you, and is it worth your while?

- Be wary of forming partnerships in situations that will allow your rival to benefit at your expense, gaining the resources to out-compete you in other areas of the industry.

- Structure and plan the partnership process carefully – negotiation, communication, and integration are vital, especially in the initial stages of an alliance.

- Be ready to expand the alliance to a range of other companies when desirable to do so.

IDEA 30
Bumper-sticker strategy

A firm should be able to summarize its business and approach in a single concise statement.

The idea

Quick and effective communication is viewed by many as a cornerstone of modern business. In light of this, it seems natural that many organizations have developed a way of summing up the most important aspects of their business in a memorable and impressive "bumper-sticker" tagline. Notable examples of organizations that use this tactic include:

- *Virgin*: "Debunk the establishment, business as fun." This statement reinforces the company's image as rebellious, confident, and daring within the corporate world.

- *BMW*: "The ultimate driving machine." Underlining its status as the most superior luxury car, BMW strives to appear as the most impressive option in a competitive market where status is vital.

- *Federal Express*: "Guaranteed overnight delivery." Showing off its core competency and proposition in three words, this statement reminds customers of its reliability and speed, while reminding employees of the importance of timely delivery.

The benefits of a good bumper-sticker slogan are not just in winning over customers – it can be useful for communicating with employees too. While the examples mentioned were for entire companies, they can be used at all levels within an organization, and adjusted for different teams, departments, and strategic initiatives. This helps teams work together towards a common goal, as well as clarifying complex sales campaigns so they can be fully understood. Bumper stickers also help sales people understand which points to emphasize.

Customer-focused taglines cement your brand's image among your consumer base, capture their attention, and remind them of the quality of your services. Make sure you have one for your business or job.

In practice

- Decide which specific aspects of your product offering or corporate strategy should be emphasized in the tagline.

- Work it into your company's advertising, wherever possible. It should come to be symbolic of your firm's values and services.

- Show a clear differentiation from your competitor.

- Promise value. See it from the customer's point of view – have you clearly outlined the advantages for them?

- Consider what is unique about your business organization that will allow you to carry out the strategy in a superior way to your competitors.

- Ensure employees are committed to the goal and take it to heart.

IDEA 31
Valuing instinct

Personal qualities such as instinct, experience, and intuition can be used to defy market research and create a previously untapped niche in the market.

The idea

Market research is often hailed as the main factor that should drive decision making. However, instinct, personal experience, and intuition are just as vital, especially in difficult times.

This was recognized by Bob Lutz who, as president of Chrysler during the late 1980s, found sales in the USA and abroad weakening. Critics claimed the organization was uninspired and lagging behind competitors. Bob Lutz believed the answer was to develop an innovative, exciting car. Stylish, with a powerful ten-cylinder engine and five-speed manual transmission, the Dodge Viper was given a premium price of US$50,000. Many advised that no US-made car would become popular at such a high price, and that the investment would be better spent elsewhere. Lutz's idea was based on nothing more than personal instinct, without any significant market research. He had to overcome considerable internal opposition, as this approach to decision making was not typical at Chrysler. However, the Dodge Viper proved to be a massive commercial success, even appearing in a number of video games as an elite racing car. It changed the public's perception of Chrysler, halted the company's decline, and boosted morale.

Bob Lutz's belief that the radically different Dodge Viper was the right decision for Chrysler was a triumph of instinct over rationality. Arguably, though, the decision was entirely rational. When threatened with stagnating sales, a lackluster brand and competitive pressures, what else was there to do except throw the rule book away by innovating and connect with customers by "wowing" them? Bob Lutz may have reached his decision through instinct, but it was his experience that told him which rules to apply.

In practice

- Differentiate yourself from competitors by basing decisions on personal experience and instinct rather than typical market research or other rational methods.

- Do not be afraid to undertake bold decisions when drastic action is required.

- Talk with people – colleagues, customers, commentators, and people in other industries. Explore their views and ideas.

- Ensure the idea is executed methodically and efficiently.

IDEA 32
Building a learning organization

Being open and keen to learn, develop, and improve is a defining characteristic of a successful leader. It is also a common feature of a successful, dynamic organization – but what does it really mean?

The idea

Beware organizations that feel a need to proudly tell you about their character: they may be speaking too soon, or just too much. For example, Enron had posters proudly announcing its integrity right up to the moment its senior managers were indicted and implicated in one of the worst ever corporate scandals. Similarly, when a politician (or anyone) says "Trust me," that's usually the last thing you would want to do.

To its great credit, one business that probably does not think of itself as a learning organization is the international publisher Pearson, yet that is exactly what it is becoming. Pearson has a host of impressive, world-class brands (including the *Financial Times* and Penguin), and this ensures it can invariably attract the brightest and the best. Yet despite its great heritage, brands, and people, there is no air of complacency, just a keenness to learn, and a tireless desire to collaborate, develop and improve. Working with

Pearson is a little like working with an Olympic athlete: it is good and it knows what it can accomplish, but it is still striving hard to get even better and do even more. This is a fundamental aspect of great organizations, yet it can often be lost or forgotten, with potentially disastrous results.

Being a learning organization, however, means more than just wanting to improve. Renowned business writer Peter Senge views a learning organization as one "Where people continually expand their capacity to create the results they truly desire, where new and expansive patterns of thinking are nurtured, where collective aspiration is set free, and where people are continually learning to see the whole together."

In practice

Senge believes that five disciplines are central to learning organizations. Consider which of these five vital aspects of learning could be improved within your business:

1. *Systems thinking* is the ability to comprehend and address the whole, understanding the interrelationship between the parts. One of the key problems with many businesses is that they apply simplistic frameworks to what are complex systems. We tend to focus on the parts rather than seeing the whole, and fail to see organization as a dynamic process. So a better appreciation of systems will lead to more appropriate action.

2. *Personal mastery* is the ability to clarify our personal vision, focus our energies, be patient, and display objectivity. People with a high level of personal mastery are continually learning, they are acutely aware of their ignorance and their growth areas, and yet they are also deeply self-confident. This seems paradoxical, but for people with personal mastery the journey is seen as the reward.

3. *Mental models* are deeply ingrained assumptions, generalizations, and views that influence how we understand the world

and how we act. Using mental models starts with looking in the mirror: learning to unearth our internal pictures of the world, bringing them to the surface, and holding them rigorously to scrutiny. It also includes the ability to carry on "learningful" conversations that balance inquiry and advocacy, where people expose their own thinking effectively and make that thinking open to the influence of others.

4. *Building a shared vision* means developing a shared picture of the future. Such a vision has the power to be uplifting, encouraging experimentation and innovation. Crucially, it can also foster a long-term perspective. What is needed for success, however, is an ability to translate a vision into a clear, practical set of principles and guiding practices.

5. *Team learning* is the final aspect of organizational learning, and is defined by Senge as "the process of aligning and developing the capacities of a team to create the results its members truly desire." It builds on personal mastery and shared vision, and recognizes that people need to be able to act together. When teams learn together, Peter Senge suggests, not only can there be good results for the organization, members will develop their skills more rapidly.

IDEA 33
Reinvention

By reviewing, rethinking, and adding flare to existing services, it is possible to develop successful aspects of a business idea while replacing others with dramatic new enhancements. In this way, old services can be reinvented, and consumers can be kept longer and sold more.

The idea

Innovation doesn't have to be all about invention. A healthy dose of reinvention can drastically alter a market and change customers' expectations. By analyzing familiar operations and experimenting with and improving the formula, it is possible to radically alter key areas of the business model while still maintaining core aspects of the formula's original appeal.

This spirit of reinvention is evident in a recent project by the Vauxhall-sponsored group of experts in style, design, and technology – known as the VXCollective. The creative collective is aiming to create the "service station of the future" – a roadside stop that provides environmentally friendly fuels, gourmet food, and attractive interior design. This marks a clear departure from traditional UK roadside service stations, visited mainly for their "greasy spoon" food outlets and restroom facilities. While the VXCollective is taking a distinctly fresh look at this formula and aiming at a broad customer base, it is maintaining the key aspects of the business model:

occupying a busy roadside location to provide refreshment and fuel to travelers.

Although this project is still in its early stages with many practical hurdles to overcome, it highlights the idea that a new approach and new style can breathe new life into an old and long-established formula.

In practice

- Decide exactly which aspects to keep and what you want to change.

- Decide whether you wish to alter the formula to appeal to a new target market, or whether you wish to simply make it more attractive to the existing market.

- Put careful thought into why you are making a particular change and how it will appeal to its target market.

- Market research can be a rich source of ideas for reinvention. What do customers dislike about the existing services available to them, and what alterations would they most want to see?

- Be clear about the business impact and benefits, as well as understanding what needs to be done to ensure success.

IDEA 34
Corporate social responsibility

By making decisions that take into account potential social and environmental issues, companies can increase their popularity and revenue while decreasing hostility from regulators and local communities.

The idea

Although the benefits of corporate social responsibility (CSR) have long been known by community-minded companies, recent years have seen a dramatic increase in businesses focusing on their social responsibility, with everyone from organic food companies to clothes retailers realizing the advantages of being welcomed and accepted in the communities they serve.

Organizations such as the Co-operative Group and cosmetics retailer The Body Shop have built their businesses on a foundation of CSR. Consequently, they have gained a strong reputation of "ethical" business practices that differentiates their brand. Other companies such as oil firms and tobacco companies that have traditionally been associated with issues such as pollution or ill health have engaged in overt ethical initiatives. However, unless these initiatives are sincerely reflected throughout the organization they can be no more than a publicity stunt to divert attention from unpopular activities.

CSR can provide companies with a "licence to operate." By acting as good corporate citizens they can avoid interference from governments and ensure they remain welcome. It has become an essential element of risk management strategy – a well-respected brand cultivated over decades can be destroyed rapidly by a CSR scandal.

In addition to persuading society of your ethical credentials, CSR can build your reputation for integrity and best practice. It is also a powerful tool to ensure employees have a strong personal commitment to your organization, as well as providing a competitive edge when recruiting new workers in a competitive job market. In this way, you can attract the best workers to maintain your corporate ethics in the future. However, CSR is not a quick fix: firms should not do it for narrow commercial gain, they should do it because they believe in it, and in the end we all benefit.

In practice

- Make the most of your CSR initiatives by surrounding them with publicity – emphasize your credentials and the depth of your approach.

- If you are unable to make large and grand gestures in the name of CSR, remember that even small initiatives can still be surprisingly valuable.

- Conduct market research to understand the ethical issues that are most significant.

- Carry out general research of your industry and location – remain in touch with the concerns of governments, local citizens, and the current social climate.

- Subject your business to a thorough, in-depth analysis. It may be possible that you are causing harm to society without intending (or even realizing) that you are.

- Be aware of cultural differences. What some societies consider to be an ethical practice, other cultures may find questionable.

- Above all, practice what you preach. If your organization talks about being socially responsible, it is essential to follow through.

IDEA 35
The tipping point

The spread of products or ideas and the decline of others are rarely understood. Writer Malcolm Gladwell has developed the idea of the "tipping point": a compelling theory about how an idea becomes an epidemic. The "tipping point" is the dramatic moment when everything changes simultaneously because a threshold has been crossed – although the situation might have been building for some time.

The idea

Malcolm Gladwell likens rapid growth, decline, and coincidence to epidemics. Ideas are "infectious," fashions represent "outbreaks," and new ideas and products are "viruses." Gladwell explains how a factor "tips" – when a critical mass "catches" the infection, and passes it on. This is when a shoe becomes a "fashion craze," social smoking becomes "addiction," and crime becomes a "wave." Advertising is a way of infecting others.

Several factors are significant in making sure that an idea "tips":

1. *The law of the few.* Epidemics only need a small number of people to infect many others. This is apparent with the spread of disease: it is the few people that socialize and travel the most that make the difference between a local outbreak and a global pandemic. Similarly, word of mouth is a critical form of communication: those that speak the most (and the best) create epidemics of ideas.

There are three types of people: connectors, mavens, and salespeople.

- *Connectors* bring people together, using their social skills to make connections. They are key agents in the spread of epidemics, as they communicate throughout different "networks" of people. Masters of the "weak tie" (a friendly, superficial connection) can spread ideas far.
- *Mavens* – information specialists – also connect with people, but focus on the needs of others rather than on their own needs, and have the most to say. Examples of mavens include teachers.
- *Salespeople* concentrate on the relationship, not the message. Their "sales" skills, with mastery of non-verbal communication and "motor mimicry" (imitating the person's emotions and behavior to gain trust), affords them a pivotal role in persuading others.

2. *The stickiness factor*. With products or ideas, how attractive they are matters as much as how they are communicated in determining whether they spread. To reach a tipping point, ideas have to be compelling and "sticky." (If something is unattractive, it will be rejected irrespective of how it is transmitted.) The information age has created a stickiness problem – the "clutter" of messages we face leads to products and ideas being ignored. To create epidemics, it is essential to make sure the message is not lost in this clutter, and to ensure the message is "sticky."

3. *The power of context*. Changes in the context of a message can tip an epidemic. Given that people's circumstances, or context, matter as much as their character, a tipping point can be controlled by altering the environment they live in. This has many implications for businesses, from employee performance to generating sales.

An example of the tipping point is "broken windows theory." One person, seeing a single broken window, may believe there is an absence of control and authority, making them more likely to commit crimes. In this way, small crimes invite more serious crimes, spawning a crime wave. This theory was used in New York City in the 1990s by the chief of police, William Braxton. The "zero tolerance" approach that targeted minor crime (eg fare-dodging and vandalism) led to a dramatic fall in crime overall. Although other factors may have contributed to the crime reduction, this example highlights the power of context.

In practice

- Choose a compelling, attractive proposition or idea to spread. Understand what will make it appealing and emphasize these factors to key contacts.

- Identify and develop links with key contacts – people with connections ("connectors" or networkers); people with knowledge and influence ("mavens" such as teachers or journalists), and people with influence ("salespeople" such as celebrities).

- Choose the right time to spread the idea, making sure that the environment is receptive and that the idea is relevant and timely.

- Read *The Tipping Point* by Malcolm Gladwell.

IDEA 36
Outsourcing

It is often possible for businesses to delegate non-core operations to external partners specializing in that operation. This can be cost-effective and allow firms to take advantage of a specialist company's expertise and its economies of scale.

The idea

Outsourcing is not simply purchasing services from another group: it involves a considerable degree of two-way information exchange, coordination, and trust. Out-tasking is slightly narrower – with very small segments of the production process being taken over, often on a short-term basis – but still requires mutual knowledge and communication. There are many advantages associated with outsourcing, both in cost and quality.

A specialist company will usually be able to complete the service more cheaply by negotiating supplier contracts and economies of scale. Variations in international economies and differences in exchange rates can make outsourcing more cost-efficient. Quality can also improve, as the specialist company should know how best to carry out the task.

However, when not properly handled, outsourcing can gain an organization a bad reputation. Strict quality management, diligent research, and attention to ethics are important when deciding which company to outsource to. This is demonstrated by technology firm Dell, whose outsourcing of customer service duties was alleged to have led to falling quality and customer dissatisfaction.

In practice

- Research the people you are outsourcing to – are they trustworthy and capable? What advantages do they offer?

- Be clear about the terms of the arrangement, and put in place a clear "service level agreement" (SLA) specifying the tasks that will be performed, how, when, and payment terms. Maintain quality and service standards when outsourcing.

- Communicate frequently to ensure both parties agree on targets and strategies.

- Remember that outsourcing can be a valuable opportunity to exercise corporate social responsibility.

- In some cases of international outsourcing, research the economy of the country where you are outsourcing, to ensure you are paying a fair and living wage to outsourced employees.

- Make sure you are aware of the business practices used by your outsourcing partner. Even if you are not in direct control of them, you are associated with their organization. Any negative business practices could easily result in your organization getting a bad reputation.

IDEA 37
Keeping your product offering current

Maintaining awareness of the latest market news, consumer concerns, and cutting-edge technologies will stimulate sales and build a loyal client base.

The idea

One of the most effective ways to keep your company current and cutting-edge is to cultivate an awareness of changing consumer concerns. Understanding your customer is vital to good business, but clients are not fixed in their desires. Their needs and wants change regularly, and for a variety of reasons – to claim you are truly at the forefront of your industry you must maintain knowledge of, and cater to, these changing demands.

Subaru's 2006 marketing strategy is an impressive example of this – every buyer of selected new Impreza, Forester, and Legacy models received £3,000 worth of free fuel vouchers. Customers who purchased any other model in the Subaru range received £1,000 worth of vouchers. This deal, not offered by any of its competitors, connects with the widespread global concern of rising fuel prices.

Instead of offering a traditional reduction in price to stimulate sales, Subaru understood the changing needs and concerns of its clients, and used this to create a truly enticing price incentive. By blending innovation with a willingness to react to the latest market developments, it is possible for businesses to prosper in volatile environments.

In practice

- Talk to your current and potential customers. What do they value? What are their concerns? What do they want?

- Find out what businesses in other industries are doing to attract customers.

- Ask people at all levels of your business, including the "extended family" such as retailers or distributors, how they would keep the product appealing.

- Plan a series of product enhancements and sales initiatives. A constant series of incentives to buy is better than a desperate splurge (or a complacent lack of activity).

- Be prepared to test a range of ideas and initiatives. Find out what works best, where and why, and see whether it can be replicated elsewhere.

IDEA 38
Experiential marketing

Holding gatherings to celebrate and promote your product can be a lively, effective way to get customers involved with and attached to your brand and services.

The idea

The idea of using themed parties to promote products challenges the assumption that potential customers are simply passive viewers of advertising. By actively involving customers in an "experiential" advertising event you differentiate your brand and build strong customer loyalty.

Holding a brand-themed party typically involves selecting a range of products to promote, and creating a way to integrate a sales pitch into a celebratory social event. Two famous examples of this tactic are Avon beauty parties and Ann Summers parties, where customers are invited to become salespeople and sell products to their friends in the context of a party. Party-goers try free samples and discuss the merits of different products. This creates a feeling of kinship and humor among customers rather than a feeling of being targeted by marketing – making them more receptive to purchasing products.

The sales tactic does not always have to be overt. Branded parties can simply be an opportunity to create awareness of your brand, create a buzz around your company, and entice people into buying at a later date. In 2006, Diageo, the company producing Baileys Irish Cream, hosted a series of "cocktail parties" in London nightclubs, where party-goers were given complimentary Baileys liquor and free recipes for using Baileys in cocktails and desserts.

Whether you are using branded parties to build an awareness of your company, or simply to sell products, they provide an enjoyable and effective marketing solution.

In practice

- Branded parties do not have to be aimed at just the "young and trendy" market – a range of events can be organized to cater to the preferences of your target customers.

- Ensure the event is as enjoyable and stress-free as possible, to allow attendees to form positive associations with your product.

- Provide free samples to introduce your product.

- Be original. Cutting-edge and daring ideas for corporate parties can gain large amounts of publicity.

- Consider the tone of the event, taking into account the desires of the demographic group you are appealing to and the purpose of the event.

- Maintain consistency with the company's values and overall approach.

IDEA 39
Information dashboards and monitoring performance

One of the biggest challenges in business is to avoid information overload, focusing instead on finding and using the right information, at the right time. This can be achieved using a simple "dashboard" approach.

The idea

An information dashboard is simply a set of key business indicators highlighting daily (or weekly) trends in performance and productivity.

Dashboards are an increasingly popular method of managing key aspects of a business, such as sales, from the top of the organization through to each individual. They enable people to know exactly where they are compared with the plan, and why. Consequently, dashboards measure not only results but also what activity has been done to create them.

HSBC has become more focused on customers and sales, rather than maintaining a traditional focus (common among banks) on processes and internal issues. Several of HSBC's business units have achieved this by providing sales information to employees in the form of dashboards.

Sales dashboards highlight key issues: the number of leads and their sources (highlighting what to continue leveraging and what to fix); the quality of the leads; the effectiveness of sales people at using leads and making appointments with customers, and ability to convert appointments to sales.

As well as driving sales, this dashboard approach has other advantages:

- Managers can help sales people improve performance by focusing on issues relevant to each individual.

- It promotes a sales-driven culture and focus within the team.

- It provides the pipeline numbers that measure activity and not just sales.

The information provided by dashboards means that managers know where to focus their support. They do not need to focus on salespeople whose month-to-date sales are behind if they have appointments for the rest of the month, whereas they do need to support people with no appointments booked, even if they are exceeding sales targets.

Information from the dashboard approach can be communicated widely, providing a common language and focus in an organization. For example, in HSBC Taiwan large plasma screens are provided for employees. As well as presenting key messages, themes, and news, they highlight sales information, which both informs and creates competition between individuals and teams.

In practice

■ Assess your information requirements and make information routinely, consistently, and reliably available, by asking the following questions:

- What information is needed?
- How should it be presented?
- When does it need to be supplied (timing and frequency)?
- Where does it come from? This determines the quality of information and puts facts into context.
- What restrictions are there? For example, whether some or all of the information is confidential.
- Which decisions and activities will it support? It helps if people know why information is needed.

■ Generate the right data – find out the best way to acquire information (e.g. surveys, telephone calls, meetings, and interviews).

■ Review and analyze information. Decisions come down to judgment, but quantitative statistical methods will highlight trends and anomalies, while scenario planning, modeling, and simulation are useful techniques for generating and assessing the right information.

■ Store and retrieve information, ensuring it is widely accessible, clearly labeled, and categorized. It needs to be relevant and up to date. Establish criteria for adding new information and discarding (or archiving) old, irrelevant details. The system and processes for storing and retrieving information need to be cost-effective.

■ Act on information. Three tactics are useful: monitor decisions, act methodically, and manage the constraints (in terms of time, resources, and other pressures).

IDEA 40
Flexible working

Allowing employees to be flexible about exactly where and when they work can lead to significant improvements in performance and job satisfaction.

The idea

Sophisticated laptops, wireless internet, a post-baby boomer generation demand for a healthier work–life balance, and possibly a shortage of alarm clocks, have resulted in the demand for flexible working becoming ever louder.

Advancements in technology have made the option of corporate flexibility a reality that is yet to be realized by many organizations. Telecommunications company Vodafone made the move to mobility in 2004, when it revolutionized its headquarters, creating a large, campus-like design with "break-out spaces where meetings can take place with laptops and notepads out." Employees were given laptops, mobile phones, and wireless internet to encourage flexibility. Vodafone commented, "people can even sunbathe with their laptop while they work ... even be at home and still work." The Vodafone scheme has generally been met with company-wide approval, with improvements in productivity and performance.

There has never been a better time to make the move to flexible working, as it is not just a nice idea but is becoming a necessity – for example, some countries, including the UK, have introduced compulsory flexible working rights legislation for parents. It is sensible to adapt your organization now to let the social, legal, and cultural shift towards flexible working begin working for you.

In practice

- Market your flexible working options to potential employees – this can help recruit graduates and give your company a valuable selling point when competing for the best workers.

- Flexible working does not mean sacrificing important deadlines or performance. Give your employees goals and responsibilities, not schedules.

- Job sharing, where two or more people are employed in one role part-time, can provide increased flexibility.

- Be prepared for a flatter organizational structure that can result from flexible working – open plan and fluid working environments tend to break down physical barriers and hierarchies. This can be met by resistance from senior managers.

- Manage the transition. Many workers may be wary of change, and others may be unsure of how to cope with the new challenges it brings. Educate employees on how to get the most out of the changes.

- Flexible working is not suitable for everyone. Some employees work better in an environment with an element of rigidity.

- Use it as an opportunity to decrease costs and reduce transport expenses by holding meetings via telephone and IM (instant messaging) technology.

IDEA 41
Redefine your audience

Finding new audiences for your product can allow you to broaden your sales potential and escape crowded markets.

The idea

Do you think you know who the best people are to target with your marketing? Think again. Reconsidering who may be interested in your products opens up a new world of potential customers, for the company intrepid enough to find a new audience for its advertising.

The Polish division of the brewing firm Carlsberg decided to create a beer to be marketed primarily to women. Karmi, a beer with a low alcohol content and high emphasis on flavor, was colorfully packaged and launched on International Women's Day. This was a bold move in an industry that typically focuses on selling to a male clientele, with advertising campaigns usually centering around sports sponsorship deals and scantily clad models.

This strategy of redefining your audience was also followed by UK clothing retailer Marks & Spencer, after its reputation for catering to older female clientele became insufficient to sustain its business. Marks & Spencer decided to expand into a younger, more style-focused market, and launched Per Una, a new range of clothes designed to appeal to women in their twenties and thirties. While it had traditionally emphasized comfort over style, the decision to present a fashion-forward image helped Marks & Spencer broaden its appeal – and turn around its flagging sales.

In practice

■ Seek an external view of your market – for example, by talking to customers, benchmarking with other businesses, or by appointing new employees from outside the business.

■ Focus on how you could adjust your product to appeal to a new audience.

■ Maintain the core principles of your product – while you should add new selling points to appeal to new audiences, do not discard your original ones.

■ Do not neglect your old market – maintain committed relationships with all your intended audiences.

■ Remember that it can be difficult to move into a new market, especially if that market is crowded. Choose your new audience wisely.

IDEA 42
Vendor lock-in

Developing products that are only compatible with other products in your range shuts out competitors and ensures repeat business from customers.

The idea

Being able to devise a foolproof strategy for retaining customers and maintaining a steady, reliable stream of revenues is the dream of many corporate executives. By using vendor lock-in – ensuring customers are dependent on your products and unable to move to another vendor without substantial switching costs – you can achieve this.

Gillette's razor-sharp business acumen exploits vendor lock-in. Its razor blade handles are only compatible with its brand of razor blades; consequently, its razor blades are the primary source of income. Manufacturer of electronic toothbrushes, Phillips Sonicare, also uses vendor-lock in. Its toothbrushes have an electronic base that requires a Sonicare replacement toothbrush head, ensuring customers will return to Sonicare and preventing them from switching to another manufacturer. Switching cost is the cost a consumer incurs when purchasing from a new company and is a key aspect of vendor lock-in. The higher the switching cost, the less likely a customer is to switch.

This concept is not new. Many businesses do this: printer manufacturers like Hewlett-Packard, camera companies such as Canon, coffee retailers such as Nespresso, all provide proprietary, reusable components for their products. These businesses ensure success by planning the reusable component of their products from the start. Where many attempts at vendor lock-in fail is viewing the reusable component as just an add-on. It isn't. It *is* the product, the benefit for the customer, and the profit for the business.

In practice

- Consider selling the original product for a low, eye-catching price to stimulate sales of the add-on components.

- Alternatively, consider making the "base product" expensive to persuade customers they have made an investment in your brand and deter them from switching to another company. The choice depends on your product, your market, and your customers. What would they value most?

- Offer a range of add-ons compatible with the base unit. This element of choice helps overcome consumers' fears that they are "stuck" with something of diminishing utility.

- Be aware that demand for your products will be interrelated – if demand for one decreases, demand for the partner product will decline.

- Switching cost is not always real – it can just be imagined by the customer. It can be enough simply to persuade your customers that it will be inconvenient or costly to switch to a new vendor.

- Plan your vendor lock-in strategy from the start. Clearly, this strategy works best for products that need to be regularly replaced.

IDEA 43
Turning the supply chain into a revenue chain

Agreeing to share sales revenue with suppliers allows companies to purchase goods for a lower price, increase revenue, and cope with fluctuations in customer demand.

The idea

In the 1990s, the leader of the video rental market, Blockbuster, found itself frustrated by never having enough copies of popular movies in stock to satisfy demand at peak times. The problem was that Hollywood studios charged $60 per video, while demand typically fell sharply a few weeks after release. Consequently, Blockbuster could not justify purchasing more than ten copies of a movie, leaving many customers frustrated at being unable to rent the latest videos.

To solve this dilemma, Blockbuster proposed giving film companies a share of the revenue from rental sales to secure a lower up-front price for videos. Blockbuster was able to break even on a video more quickly, and able to purchase more copies to satisfy demand – ensuring high standards of convenience for customers. The movie studios also benefited from increased tape sales and added revenue streams. By turning a supply chain into a revenue chain, Blockbuster had satisfied the film companies, the customer base, and its own bottom line.

In practice

- For this idea to work for your company, the incremental revenue generated by additional units must be less than the cost of producing them.

- Administrative costs should be low so they do not use up the increased profits from the scheme.

- If there is a high degree of price elasticity in your market, the lower up-front purchasing costs negotiated through revenue-sharing should be used to lower prices, to stimulate demand.

- Use sharp negotiating skills when deciding how much revenue to share with the supplier. If production costs are low, a supplier may accept a lower revenue share than you anticipate.

- Employ reliable market research to gauge consumer demand when deciding how many units to purchase, following a revenue-sharing agreement. The new lower price can make it tempting to over-purchase.

IDEA 44
Intelligent negotiating

By learning where the pitfalls lie in negotiations, it is possible to sidestep them and ensure satisfying results that last for all involved.

The idea

Harvard Business School (HBS) professor James Sebenius specializes in the field of complex negotiations. In 1993, HBS made negotiation a required course in its MBA program, and created a negotiation department within the school.

Sebenius identified six mistakes responsible for the failure of many negotiations. By avoiding them you can negotiate your way to success. These pitfalls, outlined in *Harvard Business Review*, include:

- *Neglecting the other side's problems*. If you do not understand the problems your negotiation partner is trying to overcome, you will not be able to offer the best solution.

- *Letting price bulldoze other interests*. It is easy to focus exclusively on price. Make sure you do not ignore other important factors – such as creating a positive working relationship, goodwill, a social contract between both sides, and a deal-making process that is respectful and fair to everyone.

- *Letting positions drive out interests.* Despite the existence of opposing positions, there may be compatible interests. Rather than trying to persuade someone to abandon a particular position, it can be more productive to develop a deal that satisfies a diverse range of interests.

- *Searching too hard for common ground.* Common ground can help negotiations, but different interests can allow both sides to get something out of the deal.

- *Neglecting BATNA.* This refers to the "best alternative to a negotiated agreement": the options you will be faced with if the deal falls through. These include approaching other companies or adjusting your business model. By analyzing your prospects – and your partner's prospects – you can decide what to offer in the negotiation and when to offer it.

- *Failing to correct for skewed vision.* Two types of bias can affect negotiations – *role bias* and *partisan perceptions*. Role bias (the confirming evidence trap) is the tendency to interpret information in self-serving ways, overestimating your chances of success, while partisan perceptions (the overconfidence trap) is the propensity to glorify your own position while vilifying opponents. You can overcome these biases by placing yourself in the position of your "opponent."

In practice

- An understanding of others' desires and perspective is crucial to being able to persuade them why they should agree to your proposal. Explore their position with them.

- Research an individual or company before negotiation. Do not limit research to information immediately relevant to the deal – a broad knowledge of the industry, company goals, and market conditions the organization faces will give you extra weight in negotiations.

- Do not feel the need to be overly aggressive. Show that you are a firm negotiator, but remember that mutual understanding and establishing rapport will yield large rewards.

- Conduct a full analysis of potential agreements that allow both sides to win, without either party having to accept a loss.

IDEA 45
Complementary partnering

If your product can be partnered with another, the popularity of the other product may directly affect your sales.

The idea

A "complementary good" is a product that is often consumed alongside another product. For example, beer is a complementary good to a football game, while a travel pillow is a complementary good for a long plane journey. When the popularity of one product increases, the sales of its complementary good also increases. By producing goods that complement other products that are already (or about to be) popular, you can ensure a steady stream of demand for your product.

Some products enjoy perfect complementary status – they *have* to be consumed together, such as a lamp and a lightbulb. However, do not assume that a product is perfectly complimentary, as customers may not be completely locked in to the product. For example, although motorists may seem obliged to purchase petrol to run their cars, they can switch to electric cars.

While for some industries producing complementary goods is an optional way to increase revenue, in others it is a compulsory step to avoid becoming obsolete. Producers of video games have to ensure their games are compatible with the latest consoles, while technology firms have to ensure their software programs are compatible with the latest computers and operating systems.

Advertising strategy can be geared towards the complementary status of a product – for example, beer companies sponsor football matches. This was taken to a new level in the 2006 World Cup, when FIFA officials demanded that Holland supporters remove trousers bearing the logo of Dutch beer "Bavaria," as it was a rival company to Budweiser, which was a major sponsor. While this attracted criticism for being "ambush marketing" and was probably an overly aggressive strategy, it demonstrated a corporation firmly holding on to its status as the leading complementary good.

In practice

- Be aware of possible future trends in a market. If you can anticipate a product becoming popular, you can develop a complementary product and gain first-mover advantage.

- Consider timing the release of a new product or marketing campaign to coincide with an increase in the popularity of a complementary product.

- It is dangerous merely to enjoy the success of a complementary product and stop behaving competitively. If you stop delivering high standards and reasonable prices, customers will often develop ingenious ways to find an alternative.

- Try not to produce a complementary good for a product that already has a surplus of complementary products; the competition makes it difficult to gain a foothold. For example, pretzels go with beer, but so do many other products. You won't necessarily sell more pretzels if more beer is sold.

- Your product does not have to simply complement another consumer good, it can complement a social event, seasonal weather, or other factors.

IDEA 46
Feel-good advertising

Rather than simply presenting customers with a manifesto of reasons to purchase your product, try to entertain, intrigue, or reassure them.

The idea

It can be tempting when creating an advertising campaign just to focus on why your product is superior and how you can persuade customers to purchase it. But the reality is that most of the people you reach with your advertising will be cynical and overloaded with other campaigns. Consequently, they have little interest in an unsolicited, short statement about why your product is better. This means you should find a new way of talking to them. Creating a marketing campaign that potential customers find amusing, fascinating, or heart-warming will help you reach even the most jaded consumer.

Mobile phone company Orange devised its "Orange Wednesdays" offer of free cinema tickets for customers, through a series of adverts that aired before films in the UK, which humorously lampooned the movie and advertising industries. The short clips showed movie stars unsuccessfully attempting to pitch ideas to an "Orange Film Commission," only to be shot down because the films did not do enough to promote Orange mobile telephones. Over-the-top and deliberately laughable suggestions were made to the aspiring film-makers, including "making the fourth in the trilogy" for *Lord of the Rings*, and renaming it "Lord of the Ring Tone." These non-traditional adverts satirized advertising, while subtly attempting to win customers and form positive brand associations.

Dove, a leading provider of skin and hair care products implemented a feel-good advertising promotion with its "Campaign for Real Beauty." Straying from the typical approach of cosmetic companies using attractive models, Dove encouraged customers to feel happy about the way they look naturally. Using models with a "realistic" appearance, Dove encouraged women to have a positive body image regardless of conventional beauty standards. UK newspaper *The Times* commented on the campaign: "Dove presents a refreshing antidote to the jaundiced narcissism of the professional supermodel hired to sell beauty products."

By rebelling against some of the negative or traditional practices in advertising, Dove and Orange created goodwill and positive brand awareness, while entertaining and amusing potential customers.

So don't just make your customers feel better about your product, make them feel better about themselves.

In practice

- Understand the sense of humor, social concerns, and typical "personality" of your target market.

- Consider involving entertainers in your ad campaigns to provide a memorable comic edge.

- Integrate any corporate social initiatives your company is undertaking into your advertising campaign.

- Do not feel pressured to fit your product into conventional advertising. Be critical and adapt your marketing into a more lively and customer-focused offering.

IDEA 47
Innovations in day-to-day convenience

Everyday life provides people with a large number of small challenges. By considering potential solutions to these challenges, it is possible to develop a new product that will be used regularly by many people.

The idea

Creating innovative products for day-to-day convenience combines the financial benefits of being a first mover with the reward of creating a product that is used every day by many people.

An example of an innovation in day-to-day convenience occurred in 1938, when Lazlo Biro, while working as a journalist, noticed that the ink used in newspaper printing dried quickly. He worked with his brother, the chemist Georg Biro, to produce a pen with a rotating socket that picked up ink as it moved. The BIC version of this innovation is now a ubiquitous possession, with 14 million pens sold *every day*.

Another example of the drive for everyday convenience is the BlackBerry device. The BlackBerry first made headway into the mobile communications market by concentrating on a portable email device, but now incorporates text messaging, mobile telephone, web browsing, and other wireless services. An impressive participant in the all-in-one convenience trend in modern technology, the BlackBerry is now a common reference in popular culture and a favorite of business people across the world. However, it is possible that BlackBerry did not innovate as far as it could have, with a storm of legal controversy surrounding originality. Regardless of this, both Biro and BlackBerry provide an important lesson: push creativity to its limits and find a way to provide simple, ubiquitous convenience.

In practice

- Try to design products with a focus on ease of use.

- Focus on the time-saving potential of the idea.

- Consider using deep-dive prototyping to develop, improve, and test the product.

- Don't view things as impossible – consider how you can achieve things, not whether you can.

- Consider your everyday life – what products would you most like to see enter the market?

- Observe existing products and decide how they can be more convenient and user-friendly.

- Ensure you patent your inventions as soon as possible.

IDEA 48
Lifestyle brands

By making your brand synonymous with the hobbies and aspirations of a particular cultural movement you can massively increase the appeal of your product.

The idea

It is one thing to have a well-respected brand. It is another thing entirely to have a brand that encapsulates an entire culture, identity, and lifestyle. Brands that achieve this are known as "lifestyle brands."

Used by customers to show membership of a particular cultural movement, lifestyle brands can be a form of wordless communication within society. They can also reinforce consumers' esteem and perception of themselves.

Two areas that lifestyle brands draw on are national identity and subcultures. Lingerie retailer Victoria's Secret sought in its early marketing campaigns to evoke the British upper class. Likewise, successful luxury lifestyle brand Louis Vuitton draws on the opulent image of the French aristocracy.

Subcultures – particularly in music and sport – lend themselves well to lifestyle brands. Surf and sport brand Quiksilver embodies the modern lifestyle brand. Retailing clothes, wetsuits, surfwear, and sunglasses, it has created sponsorship deals with 500 board sport professionals. To promote its presence in the surfing lifestyle, it sponsors the annual elite Quiksilver Pro tournament. All of this effort has paid off: it is a market leader in the surfing industry, a trendy fashion label for surfers and non-surfers, and a member of the Fortune 1000. When customers buy Quiksilver apparel, they are buying a lifestyle of sun, sea, and surf, without the worry of having to brave any killer waves. Your product need not be sold just for its functional use: it can be marketed as an entry fee to the life your customers desire.

In practice

- Provide sponsorship deals, to show you are aligned with the culture you wish your brand to embody.

- Placement of marketing is vital. Make your brand's presence known at appropriate festivals, tournaments, meetings, parties, and cultural hotspots.

- Sell a range of products involved with the culture – this will broaden your appeal and increase credibility.

- Subcultures are a good target for lifestyle brands, as they often feel a strong need to assert their group identity.

- Elite cultures are also suited to lifestyle brands.

- One factor is often overlooked when creating a lifestyle brand: ensure your product offering is compatible with the "lifestyle" you are promoting. If you want to market your organization as an elite sporting brand, remember to actually sell quality sporting equipment that matches the needs and perceptions of the target market.

IDEA 49
Being honest with customers

Focusing exclusively on the threat from competing businesses can leave clients feeling alienated and neglected.

The idea

In the early 1980s, soft drinks giant Coca-Cola was concerned by its decreasing market share and rivalry with the soda multinational, PepsiCo. The 1980s was a decade that saw a "taste explosion" in the soft drinks market, with the introduction of a wide range of new citrus, diet, and caffeine-free colas. Coke was being outperformed by Pepsi in a series of "blind taste tests."

Rather than focusing on the overall issue of declining popularity, Coca-Cola zeroed in on the issue of losing in the taste tests, ignoring the significance of its image, and consumer attachment to its brand. It launched "New Coke" with a new and improved taste. Although the launch technically went well, Coca-Cola soon found itself facing an angry and emotional reaction to its new formula and image. Thousands of calls were received from people wanting a return to Coke's classic product. Some of the calls were not even from Coke drinkers, but simply Americans wanting a return to a classic cultural symbol. The original Coke was brought back, Coke apologized, and the lessons were learnt. Focusing on the threat from an increased number of rivals and on Pepsi's superiority in taste tests meant Coca-Cola had lost sight of the arbiter of competition: the customer.

Making decisions based solely on the actions of competitors, without first researching what matters most to customers, can lead to serious corporate blunders.

In practice

- Work hard constantly to understand as much as possible about your customers; take great care if you are reducing their views to a few simple truths.

- Talk with customers and take every opportunity to engage with them.

- Look at the nature and history of your company: by understanding your brand and product, it is possible to gain an insight into your prospective customer base.

- Use trial launches before significant changes to your product; this reveals potential customer complaints.

IDEA 50
Instant recognizability

Creating a distinctively packaged product will secure it a lasting place in the memory of customers, convey an image, and ensure it stands out among other choices, making it easy for people to recognize instantly.

The idea

How to successfully differentiate your product is a much-debated issue in marketing and product development departments. While superior levels of customer service and quality are important, it should be recognized that people can be visually reliant when forming a first impression of a product. Consequently, packaging your product in an appealing and instantly recognizable way provides a valuable head start in the battle for differentiation.

The flat-sided, sapphire-colored bottle used to market Bombay Sapphire dry gin is instantly recognizable thanks to its striking, translucent design. It can be recognized without having to see the product name on the bottle. With this bold, style-savvy approach, potential customers are instantly drawn to the product and their curiosity piqued. Should customers wish to buy the product again, they can find it quickly and easily in an array of cleverly packaged choices. The dry gin manufacturer emphasized its design credentials by awarding the Bombay Sapphire Prize – the world's biggest international glass design award. By taking design seriously, it pushed itself further towards pole position in its market.

It is a tactic used by Coca-Cola, whose distinctively curvy, long-necked glass bottle wrapped in the distinctive red and white logo is a symbol of US consumer culture – instantly recognizable on the crowded soft drinks shelves in supermarkets.

Possessing a distinctive design allows people to form emotional attachments to your product and to use it as a status symbol. Your packaging becomes an extension of your logo – don't neglect it, and don't be content to merely conform to the industry standard, seek to surpass it.

In practice

- Pay attention to small details in product design: well-crafted lines and curves have a subtle impact.

- Sexuality can be important. Products with a design that loosely mirror the shape and form of the female body (such as a Coke bottle) are supposedly more appealing (they may make a talking point, providing an added dimension to marketing).

- Intangible products, such as financial advice, are not excluded from the challenges of good product design. Managing the customer experience and designing offices and marketing campaigns are activities that benefit from good product design to make these products and services more eye-catching, enjoyable, and memorable.

- Consider hiring a professional product expert for advice on what design will best work for your customer offering.

IDEA 51
Managing a turnaround

Undergoing a corporate transformation is fraught with danger, but guidelines can be used to make sure that it goes to plan and your organization gets the most out of the change.

The idea

Robert Reisner, former vice president of strategic planning for the US Postal Service, is well placed to talk about the pitfalls of managing organizational change. Amid soaring profits in 1999, the US Postal Service made an attempt to revolutionize its business technologically to allow it to compete in a new "wired" era. Although this effort to better integrate into a technologically advanced society was met with initial optimism, it soon began to stall. In 2001, the company was facing a $3 billion loss, motivation was falling, and the General Accounting Office described the turnaround as having a "high chance of failing."

Reisner identified key steps that led to the transition stalling, which provide important lessons for corporate transformation:

1. *Not missing your moment*. Time your change initiatives to coincide with market opportunities and high morale among employees.

2. *Connecting the transformation with the core of your business*. Make sure employees understand how the changes are relevant to the mainstream operations of the company.

3. *Telling the difference between incremental improvements and strategic transformation*. Don't let temporary business success distract from the need for a strategic reinvention.

4. *Setting realistic goals*. Creating unrealistic expectations is detrimental to the motivation of employees and managers, and distracts from the goals that can be achieved.

Although you can never guarantee that a major business transformation will proceed as planned, you can guarantee that you will be prepared to deal with the challenges it presents, and to navigate your way around them.

In practice

- Help employees deal with the stress they face during the transformation.

- Take advantage of the contributions that current employees can make to the turnaround.

- Create lists of what needs to be done, communicate priorities, and implement the changes.

- Focus on one initiative at a time – trying to do too much will overwhelm your organization.

- Take control of the situation by asking productive, practical questions on how to make the transition succeed.

IDEA 52
Diversity

To remain competitive in an increasingly global society, you need to have a diverse range of employees working at all levels. Diversity is about difference; companies which bring to bear different experiences and perspectives stand a greater chance of success in an increasingly global market than those which cannot.

The idea

Society is far from homogenous; with steep increases in the popularity of global trade, this also applies to the majority of industries and markets. Embracing a diverse approach helps attract and retain the most skilled employees, and will allow your company to benefit from a varied pool of ideas and experiences. It is a necessary step in enabling your company to relate to, communicate with, and service a diverse range of customers. Diversity also has strong links with increased productivity, innovative thinking, and lowered risks.

Seeking to reconcile the relationship between the marketplace and the workplace, IBM created a Global Diversity Council to deal with issues such as multicultural awareness and tolerance, advancement of women, integration of people with disabilities, and creating a diverse managerial team. J.T. Childs, vice president of the Global Workforce for Diversity, commented, "Leadership for diversity at the top remains an IBM tradition."

By embracing this idea, your organization can reflect the

diversity of the markets it serves, and show commitment to a more diverse, valuable, and enduring group of customers.

In practice

- If you have a diverse workforce but a homogenous group of top-level decision makers, your organization will not benefit fully from diversity. Top-level commitment and example are vital.

- Find ways to encourage a culture of inclusion, respect, and communication among all employees.

- Use yourself as a role model within the business for successfully dealing with diversity.

- Recognize the difference between superficial diversity (e.g. differences in gender and ethnicity) and deep-level diversity (eg. differences in knowledge and differences in values). Encourage your organization to embrace both types of diversity.

IDEA 53
Balancing core and the context

Core activities are the unique skills that differentiate an organization from its competitors and persuade customers of its superiority. Context activities are the processes needed to meet the industry standard, without surpassing it. Getting the balance right between the two is essential for keeping focused on the right things – it is surprisingly tricky.

The idea

Core activities are known as *business idea factors*, while context activities refer to *hygiene factors*. For example, a core activity for Microsoft might be its ability to develop new software, whereas context (hygiene) factors include its ability to process orders and dispatch products. Both are vital, but only one (the core) is where the real value of the business lies.

Shareholders typically want to concentrate on core activities, as these tend to raise share prices. Also, it is possible for businesses to become too involved in the hassle of context activities and lose focus on what differentiates them. Catering to context activities is vital for remaining in a market, while focusing on core activities grows business and increases competitive advantage.

Business strategist Geoffrey Moore recommends balancing core and context by outsourcing or automating context activities. In this way, you can ensure context activities are being handled competently, are cost-effective, and are enjoying the economies of scale of a specialist company. Another benefit is the ability to devote increased investment to gaining a competitive edge within your market.

Many companies, including Cisco, Dell, General Motors, IBM, and Kodak, have outsourced their context processes to allow their organizations to cope with both core and context demands. Sabrix, a leading provider of software for managing taxation, outsourced context processes, with company president and CEO Steve Adams stating: "Outsourcing human resources and parts of our financial IT system has allowed us to keep the right people focused on the right things – things that differentiate our company." Instead of devoting key employees to working in IT and HR infrastructure, Sabrix was able to focus talented employees on reaching new levels in tax research, software development, and customer support: the core activities for Sabrix.

In practice

- Be clear about what is core and what is context. Recognize that some of these activities might be dynamic, moving between categories.

- Be prepared to overcome possible resistance to outsourcing initiatives and the rearranging of managerial responsibility.

- Delegate core activities from top management to middle management, as they will have a better view of market trends. By delegating responsibility to different parties, you can ensure that no level within the organization becomes overwhelmed.

- Encourage top-level support to outsourcing and managing context activities.

IDEA 54
Business process redesign

Rethinking and overhauling your business processes can lead to increases in revenue, reliability, cost efficiency, and quality.

The idea

Michael Hammer and James Champy, who helped introduce business process redesign (BPR), described it as "the analysis and design of workflow and processes within and between organizations." When an organization is facing difficulties or simply not operating at maximum efficiency, BPR can help it regain a competitive edge.

General Motors, one of the world's largest auto manufacturers, underwent a three-year BPR program to consolidate its multiple desktop systems into one efficient system. Donald G. Hedeen, director of desktops and deployment at GM and manager of the upgrade program, stated that the BPR "laid the foundation for the implementation of a common business communication strategy across General Motors." Although it was not cheap – technology companies Lotus and Hewlett-Packard received their largest non-governmental orders ever from GM during the process – it yielded significant benefits, with supposed savings of 10 percent to 25 percent on support costs, 3 percent to 5 percent on hardware, and 40 percent to 60 percent on software licensing fees. GM also gained heightened efficiency by over-coming incompatibility issues by using only one platform throughout the entire company.

Although BPR processes have yielded significant results for leading companies, including Procter & Gamble, Southwest Airlines, and Dell, certain businesses have used the term BPR to explain and excuse large-scale and unpopular job cuts. This has resulted in a negative reputation among some, but it is possible to carry out a BPR program that is sensitive to employee needs and effective for the business.

After the primary targets and areas of focus for your organization have been decided, key areas for consideration when designing BPR include how to reach maximum efficiency, achieve the intended results of the redesign, measure performance, and reward employees.

In practice

- Successful BPR typically includes five stages:
  1. Determining whether a BPR is actually necessary. Analyze the scope and resources that a redesign requires, and the structural and organizational challenges that are likely to be encountered, to decide whether a redesign is appropriate and viable.
  2. Creating a comprehensive and structured strategy for your BPR before undertaking it.
  3. Redesigning the structure of your primary processes, with a focus on efficiency.
  4. Putting in place a management team to direct the process, oversee the transition, and measure success.
  5. Implementing and integrating the BPR, successfully managing the changes that result.

- Effectively manage all people involved with, and affected by, your BPR. They are in charge of the success of the project and are the most unpredictable factor.

- Avoid being tempted to focus too heavily on automation – this can be unpopular and deprive your business of the "human factor."

- Create contingency plans should the BPR have unintended consequences.

- Avoid common BPR pitfalls, such as problems with managerial incompetence, lack of support, and offloading the entire restructuring process to the IT department.

- Do not create unrealistic expectations – be practical about what BPR can accomplish.

IDEA 55
Convergence

In certain instances, the entry requirements for different markets become very similar, enabling firms to participate easily in multiple industries, spreading risk and gaining benefits of scale.

The idea

As companies grow and establish themselves, they typically acquire a significant number of assets. These factors of production (such as employees, land, or machinery) may have multiple uses, allowing them to be used to produce a variety of products in a cost-effective way. In this way, a valuable competitive edge can be gained when entering new markets.

This tactic was employed by a large number of utility companies in the 1980s and 1990s which, following industry deregulation, realized they had the means of production to operate in the gas, electricity, telephone, and water markets simultaneously. They put their large number of core competencies – including call centers, advanced metering and billing services, and maintenance vehicles – to full use in a variety of markets, increasing their efficiency and turnover.

Are you certain your organization is doing all it can to serve customers, using all the resources at its disposal? By recognizing all the possible uses of assets, an organization can get the most from its resources, spread financial risk, and increase convenience for customers.

In practice

- Customer loyalty and a trusted reputation are valuable resources that can ensure your success when deciding to offer new services.

- Take full advantage of convergence by cross-selling products to customers.

- Hire specialists with expertise in the market you wish to enter; just because your firm is successful in one industry does not guarantee success in another.

IDEA 56
Cross-selling and up-selling

Cross-selling means selling additional products to a customer who has already purchased (or signaled their intention to purchase) a product. Cross-selling helps to increase the customer's reliance on the company and to decrease the likelihood of the customer switching to a competitor.

The idea

An idea that first gained momentum in the 1980s, cross-selling involves firms offering a variety of products and services to customers, then using an integrated selling process to market this range to existing clients. For example, if customers trust a firm to provide them with health insurance, they may also trust it to provide car insurance. The company can take advantage of this trust by offering both services, and targeting existing customers with marketing schemes.

Internet-based travel agent Expedia offers an impressively seamless and effective example of cross-selling. When customers complete an online order for a hotel or plane ticket, they are presented with a webpage offering them the opportunity to purchase car hire. Low-cost European airline Easyjet uses cross-selling on its website, for example, by offering travel insurance to customers in the process of purchasing a ticket.

However, smaller businesses and offline companies needn't be put off; cross-selling does not need to be a technologically advanced process. Simple integrated sales pitches can be just as effective. For example, having salespeople mention products when taking an order can encourage customers to make multiple purchases.

Cross-selling is similar to up-selling, although there are some key differences. Up-selling is where a salesperson attempts to have the consumer purchase more expensive items, upgrades, or other related add-ons in an attempt to make a better sale. Up-selling usually involves marketing more profitable services or products. An example of up-selling is adding side dishes to a food order, selling an extended service contract for an appliance, or selling luxury finishing on a vehicle.

In practice

- Ensure the profit from the extra items covers the cost of the time spent selling them.

- Educate sales staff to ensure they have a full understanding of the products they are offering.

- Plan which products to offer to which customers. As with any sale, integrity and honesty (even straightforward openness) usually work best.

- Only attempt to sell products that are clearly linked to a specific purchase the customer has made. This ensures the marketing pitch is more appropriate and less opportunistic.

IDEA 57
Kotter's eight phases of change

An organization undergoing significant changes should pay attention to eight key steps to avoid the problems that typically occur.

The idea

Leadership expert John Kotter studied 100 companies going through transitions. By analyzing their triumphs and pitfalls, he identified a number of commonly made mistakes. This led Kotter to compile the "eight steps of change": a sequence of actions to ensure that changes succeed.

1. *Establish a sense of urgency*. Organizations frequently allow high levels of complacency to develop during times of transition. Kotter commented, "Without motivation, people won't help and the effort goes nowhere. Executives underestimate how hard it can be to drive people out of their comfort zones." To accept change, businesses need a "burning platform" to remove complacency and inertia.

2. *Form a strong guiding coalition*. A group of strong, unified leaders should drive the change process and establish support throughout the entire organization.

3. *Create a vision*. A clear sense of direction and an idea of the

end result will allow efforts to be focused, organized, and efficient.

4. *Communicate the vision.* The strategy and vision for change must be communicated to everyone involved. As well as holding discussions and using other forms of communication, members of the guiding coalition should act as role models for the type of behaviors and decisions that are needed.

5. *Empower others to act on the vision.* If old procedures and obstacles remain in place during change, it will be demotivating for employees involved in the effort. So, encourage and support people to make the right changes, ideally without always referring upwards.

6. *Plan for and create short-term victories.* Find ways to start the process and work hard to generate momentum, even in small ways. Motivate employees by continuously emphasizing milestones and successes. Accentuate the positive aspects of the transition.

7. *Consolidate improvements and maintain momentum.* Rather than growing complacent as the process develops, use the credibility gained to reinvigorate and expand the changes to all areas of the company.

8. *Institutionalize the new approaches.* Anchor the changes firmly in the culture of the organization. When changes become entrenched, they are most effective.

When planning a change process with these steps in mind, it is important to allow enough time for the full sequence of events and to carry them out in the correct order. Kotter discovered that following the change plan sequentially and patiently was fundamental to success: "Skipping steps creates only the illusion of speed and never produces satisfactory results. Making critical mistakes in any of the phases can have a devastating impact, slowing momentum and negating hard-won gains."

In practice

■ Ensure your change process has both a leader, to align, motivate, and inspire the workforce, and a manager, to make a complex set of processes run smoothly and according to plan.

■ Create a clear vision of the process, as well as a sequence of events that will occur, and communicate this throughout your organization.

■ Paint a compelling vision of the future and produce strategies to realize this vision.

■ Understand that different types of change processes will require different skills and attributes, at different times. For example, a crisis change process may require an emphasis on strong leadership rather than management.

■ Even successful change processes are messy and do not always go according to plan – be ready to deal with the unexpected.

■ Ensure your "guiding coalition" is unified in their objectives and work as a team.

IDEA 58
Business-to-business marketing

An organization marketing products or services to other businesses (to use either in the production of their final products or to support their operations) is known as business-to-business (b2b) marketing. By differentiating this from consumer marketing you can better understand the unique demands of b2b marketing and increase the likelihood of success.

The idea

Business marketing may appear to be a small niche within the larger field of advertising. However, it is an area of surprising significance – more than $60 million is spent daily by companies such as GE, DuPont, and IBM to support their operations. Arguably, the potential of business marketing exceeds that of consumer marketing: the purchases made by businesses, government agencies, and institutions account for more than half of the economic activity in industrialized countries. As a discipline, business marketing has seen an impressive growth in popularity, with more than half of marketing majors now choosing to begin their careers in business marketing rather than consumer marketing.

In practice

To achieve success in business marketing, it is useful to understand how its methods differ from those of traditional consumer marketing:

- With b2b marketing, you are likely to be much more effective at every stage of the sale if you understand, in detail, your customers' priorities, strategy, and business.

- Whereas consumer marketing favors mass media to appeal to large target demographics, business marketing relies on smaller, more direct channels of distribution to reach a specific audience.

- A higher level of specialist industry knowledge is required when orchestrating a business marketing campaign, to target and appeal to the individual needs of a niche market.

- Personal and long-term client relationships are of particular significance when seeking to maintain lucrative supplier contracts – ongoing customer service should be emphasized.

IDEA 59
Employee value proposition

The struggle to attract bright, talented workers is increasingly challenging. Firms must devise a comprehensive, appealing perception of their organizations – and it must be genuine, delivering what it promises, or those bright employees will leave.

The idea

The balance of power has shifted from employers to employees. Daniel Pink, former chief speech writer for Al Gore, attributed this shift to "Karl Marx's revenge," with the means of production now in the hands of the workers. The internet has made it easier for potential employees to search for jobs, check expected salary levels, and find out what it is like to work within a particular organization.

While the power of employees has grown, many organizations have lost their appeal to job seekers. They no longer provide financial stability, with many firms unwilling or unable to offer job security.

In light of these shifting conditions and following research into 90 companies, the Corporate Executive Board (CEB) suggested formulating an employment value proposition (EVP) to attract the best workers. An EVP is the benefits an employee can expect to gain from working with an organization. The CEB found firms that effectively managed EVP could expect to increase their pool of potential workers by 20 percent. Surprisingly, they were also able to decrease the amount they paid to employees – organizations with successful EVPs paid 10 percent less.

With the workplace changing and the number of "free agents" increasing, it is increasingly important to develop a strategy for attracting the best. Remember, talented people need organizations less than organizations need talented people.

In practice

- Developing a successful EVP is important to organizations wishing to attract younger workers or technologically skilled workers.

- Emphasize the stimulation and value of the work your organization does, as well as the rewards and opportunities.

- Provide opportunities for employees to engage in informal training and to advance their skills.

- Encourage current and former employees to champion your organization. Many people now put more trust in word of mouth than in advertising.

- Fine tune your EVP for different sections of the job market.

- Change key aspects of the EVP for different areas of the world.

IDEA 60
Built-in obsolescence

Before you release a product, create a plan for when and how it will become obsolete. This allows you to control change in the market, prepare for it, and use it to your advantage.

The idea

The theory of "built-in obsolescence" can be described as "instilling in the buyer the desire to own something a little newer, a little better, a little sooner than is necessary." This definition highlights the underlying nature of planned obsolescence.

Obsolescence is the point where a product has become useless – from being out of fashion, outmoded, incompatible with other operating systems, or simply expired. Two types of obsolescence exist: stylistic obsolescence and functional obsolescence. These two types are not mutually exclusive – they are often interrelated and lead to each other. By planning the point at which your product becomes obsolete, you can begin developing a replacement and an accompanying marketing campaign. It is also possible to trigger obsolescence to stimulate sales and ensure you remain ahead of competitors.

The majority of products are destined to become obsolete – in some markets, such as fashion and technology, obsolescence is fast-paced and woven into the fabric of the industry. Technology firm Apple provides an impressive example of this; it frequently develops new MP3 players that are upgraded in both style and in technical features, making its older products stylistically and technically obsolete.

It is possible to use this strategy to make your competitors' products obsolete. For example, by releasing a popular new computer chip you can trigger the obsolescence of your competitors' operating systems.

Obsolescence is inevitable – use it to your advantage.

In practice

■ Avoid triggering the obsolescence of products too frequently, as this is often an unnecessary investment and may cause a consumer backlash.

■ Base the engineering of a product on your "obsolescence strategy" – a product will not need to last for ten years if it will be obsolete after two.

■ Offer long-term warranties on products that will soon become obsolete – this will reassure customers and it is unlikely the guarantees will be claimed.

■ Do not make built-in obsolescence obvious to the consumer – this will lead to frustration and unwillingness to purchase.

IDEA 61
Avoiding commoditization

When a product becomes easily interchangeable with other products of the same type, it is said to become a "commodity." The process of a previously differentiated and specialized product becoming interchangeable is known as commoditization. While it is believed to increase overall economic efficiency, it can be difficult for individual companies to handle. Economic value and profits come from scarcity, whereas commoditization can curtail the potential for profit.

The idea

A famous example of commoditization is the microchip industry. While microchips started out as a specialized innovation that commanded a high price, they gradually became mass produced and interchangeable. This commoditization altered the nature of the microchip industry, increasing competition and decreasing profit margins.

Harrah's Entertainment, a gaming corporation that operates hotels and casinos in the USA, recognized that traditional attempts made by casinos at avoiding commoditization – such as creating increasingly garish and noticeable designs – were becoming stale and ineffectual. It decided that the most effective way to avoid becoming an interchangeable commodity would be to establish an increased level of customer communication and gratification. A loyalty program was introduced where valuable customers were rewarded with significant gold, platinum, and diamond-level privileges. Harrah's CEO Gary Loveman commented, "When I started, this business was commoditized – you have a big box and gaming tables. Your challenge is to differentiate yourself from the other big boxes."

While commoditization is viewed as the largely inevitable fate of many products, companies can increase their chances of avoiding it by differentiating themselves, recognizing when commoditization is about to occur, and taking steps to ensure their product remains on the cutting edge.

In practice

- Find new ways to make your product or service distinctive, and avoid letting your product become an undifferentiated commodity.

- Ensure that some aspect of your product remains specialized, unique, and valuable for your customers.

- Consider the potential for commoditization, when deciding to invest in growth industries.

- Utilize intellectual property protection laws, and create products or services that cannot be easily mimicked by competitors.

IDEA 62
Developing employee engagement

Employee engagement is widely seen as being vital to improving business performance, effectiveness, and productivity. Researchers at Gallup identified several variables that, when satisfied, form the foundation of strong feelings of engagement (see www.gallup.com).

The idea

Business researchers at Gallup identified 12 questions measuring the effect of employee engagement, including such issues as retention, productivity, profitability, customer engagement, and safety. These questions, known as the Q^{12}, measure those factors that leaders, managers, and employees can influence. The questions are based on hundreds of interviews and focus groups, involving thousands of workers in many organizations, at all levels, across a broad range of industries and countries.

In practice

To succeed, it is best to work with a business that possesses experience of administering and delivering Gallup's Q^{12} and can advise on the key issues.

The questions below will help you focus on the challenge of increasing engagement. Consider them either for you or your team, and rate your response to each question on a scale of 1 (low) to 5 (high).

- Is the team focused on the right things? Is everyone agreed on the priorities and strategy?

- Do the business culture and processes help or hinder collaboration? What changes would improve the situation?

- How well is performance monitored? Does the business merely rely on financial indicators or are there other measures?

- Where do tensions typically arise and where are they likely to arise in the future?

- What is the best way to handle and reconcile tensions when they arise?

- Where is the team succeeding and where do we need to improve (individually, and as a team)?

- Are objectives and processes aligned, consistent and pulling in the same direction? If not, what needs to change?

- In the last seven days, have you received recognition or praise for doing good work?

- At work, do your opinions seem to count?

- In the last six months, has someone at work talked to you about your progress?

- In the last year, have you had opportunities at work to learn and grow?

IDEA 63
Managing by wandering about (MBWA)

It sounds immensely trivial, but participating with employees and observing their day-to-day activities in a friendly manner can help you to discover and solve problems, gather knowledge, and form valuable relationships.

The idea

A personable and hands-on style of management, MBWA advocates walking around departments, talking with employees, and casually observing the process of work. In this way, valuable relationships can be formed with employees and knowledge can be shared. While it normally accompanies an "open door" management approach, MBWA involves many more proactive elements, such as seeking problems through casual observation and discussion rather than waiting for employees to report them. An organization where the manager is fully integrated with their team, and aware of their attitudes and the challenges they face, will become more robust and adept at spotting potential problems ahead of competitors.

MBWA revolutionized the "ivory tower" approach of many managers and was soon adopted as part of the Hewlett-Packard (HP) Way – the open management style of successful technology business Hewlett-Packard. The HP Way soon became widely respected and mimicked by global corporations.

Care should be taken to ensure that employees do not view efforts at increased socialization and observation as an attempt to "spy on" or pick fault with their work. If they do, this will increase barriers and stress levels rather than reduce them. The solution is simple: be genuine in your interest and involvement. When done in a friendly, non-threatening manner, MBWA can carry an organization through difficult times and help managers to develop a business plan with an intimate knowledge of the people and resources that will be enacting it.

Blindingly obvious common sense? Yes. Important? Yes. Frequently overlooked and neglected? Yes.

In practice

- Be prepared to learn from employees – they are one of the most valuable sources of insight and ideas in your organization.

- Take advantage of natural opportunities to socialize, such as in communal office spaces and over drinks.

- Talk to, and build relationships with, a range of individuals with different responsibilities within your department.

- Provide practical support and be dependable, fulfilling any promises. Listen to what people say, and consider how and why they are saying it.

- Use MBWA as an opportunity to communicate, explain, encourage, discuss, and decide.

- Understand the personal requirements of team members. They are responsible for enacting company policy and it is important to be aware of their strengths and weaknesses when deciding on company strategy.

IDEA 64
Precision marketing

Decide who your ideal customers are – then decide where they go, what they do, and what they want. Use this information to target them precisely at key points in their everyday lives.

The idea

Precision marketing involves asking four questions – who, what, when, and how – to create a sharply effective marketing strategy.

ABN, a bank wishing to court wealthy Dutch customers, created a lounge at Amsterdam's Schiphol Airport for the exclusive use of its Preferred Banking clients (account holders with savings or investments exceeding €50,000, or a monthly income exceeding €5,000). The elite lounge was open daily from 6 am to 10 pm, providing meeting space, internet access, refreshments, foreign currency exchange, and a place to relax amidst the rush of traveling. With this project, ABN showed a clear understanding of precision marketing:

- *Who its customers were*: comfortably wealthy individuals traveling from the Netherlands.

- *What they wanted*: a place to enjoy relaxation and luxury when traveling.

- *When they wanted it*: between 6 in the morning and 10 in the evening, when the majority of flights depart and arrive.

- *How to deliver it*: creating an exclusive lounge that provided the amenities valued by affluent travelers.

What makes precision marketing special is its ability to reach its target audience and to meet their preferences in a memorable way, promoting a robust product that can withstand competitors.

In practice

- Make sure you target the right market by gaining access to reliable market research – for example, via web marketing. Precision is the vital element of precision marketing!

- Hold brainstorming sessions where each of the "four questions" of precision marketing are considered in depth.

- Consider what precision marketing strategy you would realistically be able to carry out that surpasses your competitors' current efforts.

- Find ways to enhance your marketing and your offer. Keep it fresh, appealing, targeted, and distinctive.

IDEA 65
Branding

The creation of a powerful and well-respected brand is the key to increasing market share and company value. Brands are key intangible resources which need to be carefully developed and maintained. Their features include reputation, trust, loyalty, and understanding among customers.

The idea

A brand is a design, name, or identity that is given to a product or service in order to differentiate it from its competitors. Customers know they can expect certain values associated with brands. For example, Rolls-Royce cars are associated with quality, reliability, and prestige, while Wal-Mart built its reputation on homely convenience and low price.

Brands are complex assets. One method of managing brands is to view them as having "personalities." This concept of brand personality highlights their power. Rolls-Royce is a brand with an almost mythical status: a byword for engineering standards that have long been met or even surpassed by others. The advantages of trusted brands are clear:

- Pricing. A successful and established brand can command a substantial price premium, exceeding the extra cost in terms of production and marketing. This derives from the element of trust that a brand provides. Research in the UK has shown that consumers are often prepared to pay 30 percent extra for a new product from a trusted brand than for one from an unnamed one.

- Distribution advantages. An established brand can ensure manufacturers get the best distributors. Distributors are more receptive to a new product from an established brand.

- Brand identity or image reinforces the product's appeal. The Rolls-Royce brand has a stately identity and is associated with values of craftsmanship, tradition, and prestige; Volvo has a different brand identity, with associated values of safety, functionality, and family orientation. The brand values of different products reinforce their appeal to specific market segments.

- Brands help to build customer loyalty, because of the trust and affection they generate.

- Brands make it easier to introduce new products by exploiting "brand equity."

- Brands provide opportunities to open up new market segments. For example, food manufacturers create sub-brands with diet versions of products.

- A strong brand enables products to overflow from one geographic market into another. This is particularly the case in industries affected by fashions.

- Brands can extend the life of a product. As brands combine trust and respect, careful marketing can exploit these qualities and inject new life into a stagnating product. For example, Danish toy maker Lego produces toys linked with films.

- Brands provide a valuable, market-oriented focus around which firms can organize themselves. The brand manager is often directly responsible for what the product offers, as well as how it appears to the customer.

In practice

■ Understand how the brand will be used. Is it to provide reassurance, to enable a premium price, or to create a desire to buy? Understand what benefits the brand offers customers, and how reliable and trustworthy it is.

■ Know what the brand means to customers, then deepen this appeal. Ensure the tone of marketing is commensurate with the brand values and target market.

■ Identify how the brand differentiates a product from competitors, to decide which attributes to emphasize.

■ Conduct an audit of the brand to determine how strong it appears to customers. This will reveal how the brand can be used in new markets.

■ Ensure there is sufficient investment in the brand, and discover how the brand can be strengthened. This active brand management will build customer value and loyalty.

IDEA 66
Empowerment

When employees at all levels of a company are empowered to make the decisions they feel are necessary, individual job satisfaction, corporate efficiency, and productivity soar.

The idea

Rosabeth Moss Kanter, Harvard Business School professor, argues that companies can improve performance by allowing employees to make decisions without constantly consulting superiors. Such empowerment releases the creative power of a team; given the right work environment and level of responsibility, people will make a much greater positive contribution.

When empowering team members you are letting them get on with the job entirely: they are both responsible and accountable, within certain agreed boundaries. Leaders need to set a clear, unambiguous direction and to ensure that people remain on course, by offering support without taking over. Empowerment involves:

- letting each member of the team get on with their job

- letting those team members closest to customers take decisions themselves

- removing obstacles and unnecessary bureaucracy

- encouraging and enabling people to put their ideas for improvement into practice.

By using empowerment, the Ritz-Carlton hotel chain improved customer service and differentiated itself from competitors. Employees were trusted to use their initiative and to access a small budget to ensure customers' specific needs and preferences were met. This provided a distinctive service and customer value at a competitive price.

In practice

- Understand what you mean by empowerment and what you want to achieve.

- Identify barriers to empowerment and how they can be overcome.

- Communicate your ideas and win support.

- Establish and agree the boundaries, and be prepared to have these boundaries tested.

- Ensure that your people have the necessary skills, resources, and attitudes to take control.

- Agree objectives and performance measures. Empowerment is not about dumping work on people and leaving them: it requires support and agreement.

- Provide support, monitor developments, and iron out any difficulties, particularly in the early days, but make sure that you do not undermine the process.

- Try to secure early "wins" and successes that highlight the value of the process.

IDEA 67
Rethinking the budget

Is budgeting an indispensable, practical tool for effective management? Or is it a corporate ritual and hassle that far outweighs any benefit it provides? There is a third view: that it is useful, but only up to a point, and that by rethinking the budget a firm can dramatically improve its financial management.

The idea

Diageo was created following the 1997 merger between Guinness and GrandMet FMCG. Following the merger, 60 finance managers from across the business met to discuss how they could best serve their shareholders in the future. Overwhelmingly, the response was to "blow up the budget." The feeling was that the budget process consumed vast resources, took too much time, and its one-size-fits-all approach took too little account of each individual business. There was little benefit for the shareholders in this detailed process (which is typical of many corporations). The budgeting exercise was seen as a game, and managers believed that shareholders were not concerned with assessing performance against arbitrarily agreed targets, but with whether the company was worth more this year than last.

There was a feeling that something had to be done – people were wasting too much time and money. The finance department began to:

- streamline the existing system

- move to an integrated strategic and annual planning process built around key performance indicators (KPIs) and, crucially, rolling forecasts

- emphasize strategy-driven KPIs rather than simply measuring performance against budget.

This ensured that people at every level and position had relevant metrics – measures of their individual and team performance – while giving the board the right information. The same data, slightly modified, enabled business units to operate productively.

Diageo preferred performance indicators that were externally oriented and forward-looking, rather than historical or internally focused measures. The result was a management focus that instead of dwelling on presentations of past figures and performance was more concerned with resolving business issues and preparing for the future.

The previously unsung talents of finance experts made this inevitable: they had more to offer than simply tallying past events. Other business leaders, and in particular shareholders, want finance personnel to help them get the greatest value from every asset – including the expertise in their finance department.

In practice

- Consider moving to a rolling budget, rather than a massive annual upheaval.

- Measure more than finances. Regularly review the issues that have a major impact on your business, such as number of customers acquired or lost, marketing effectiveness, and employee engagement and productivity.

- Gain support from the top of the business and also ensure

that the new approach is as inclusive and widely supported as possible.

- Look outside the business for information, ideas, and insight. Find expertise among people that have made their budget more dynamic, practical, and relevant.

IDEA 68
The buyer's cycle

To understand how to influence someone or to sell an idea, it is essential to know how people buy. The buyer's cycle provides a clear picture of the stages that need to be influenced to make a successful sale.

The idea

One of the factors behind the success of businesses such as Dell is their ability to understand their customers. This firm (and others) ensures that its approach is as flexible as possible and as informed as it can be. Understanding buyers' attitudes will enable you to influence behavior more easily and effectively.

Buying attitudes are determined by the buyer's perception of the immediate business situation, how your proposal is likely to change that situation, and the extent to which that change will close a gap between the current reality and future goal.

In practice

Focus on each of the stages in the buyer's cycle. Consider what you can do to influence your customers at each stage:

1. *Increase awareness*. The first challenge is to develop awareness of your business or new product among potential clients. This provides a feeling of familiarity, comfort, or intrigue. This awareness can then be used to lead customers

into the next stage: information. The potential market size at this stage is 100 percent.

2. *Provide information*. This stage is when specific details are provided to the customer. Their interest may vary from a passing willingness to find out more, to a passionate need to explore the offer. Whatever the customer's motives or situation, the information needs to be clear, useful, and specific. Inevitably, the market size will have shrunk as some "aware" customers fail to pick up the information, either through choice or circumstance.

3. *Help customers prioritize*. Customers weigh up the benefits and then prioritize their expenditure. For example, they may consider whether this is something they want to buy now, at this price, and in this form. They may also evaluate alternatives. Clearly, some people will not make the move from having the information to making a purchase.

4. *Help customers purchase*. Having decided to buy, the next step for the customer is to complete the transaction. It is important to enable the buyer to move as easily as possible through the process. Purchasing should be easy and satisfactory – even enjoyable.

5. *Support the customer's use of the product*. This is a stage that is often forgotten, hidden in the shadow of the purchase. A sale is not the end of the process because customers have to use and value their purchase. If they don't then the product may be returned, customers may stay away in future, and the resultant poor publicity and a declining reputation is likely to adversely affect future sales.

6. *Promote reuse*. This is when the product or service (or one of its components) is bought again. This generates additional revenue at a higher margin (without the cost of customer acquisition) and highlights customer loyalty to the product, resulting in a stronger sales process.

7. *Encourage advocacy*. This stage is highly prized by sellers: it occurs when customers are so impressed with their

purchase that they tell others about it (Harley-Davidson is an excellent example of this). Advocacy increases awareness of the product or business and feeds back to the first stage of the process.

IDEA 69
Direct selling

Closely linked to the buyer's cycle is the ability to sell direct to customers. Dell rose to be the best-selling computer supplier in the world by tailoring products to each individual need in a way that customers valued. Dell's approach was very simple: understanding its customers and selling direct.

The idea

Dell believes that by selling computer systems directly to customers it can best understand and meet their needs. This direct business model eliminates expensive retailers that Dell feels may diminish its understanding of customer expectations. The direct model also allows the company to build every system to order at competitive prices.

In 1988, Dell Computer started competing aggressively with the market leaders, IBM and Compaq. Dell's strategy was to provide good-quality personal computers at low (but not the lowest) prices, backed up with friendly and reliable after-sales service. But the real key to Dell's success was to carefully target this product offering by getting to know its customers in detail. Large amounts of advertising were placed in new (and unfashionable) magazines read by computer experts, raising the business's profile with this key group. Combined with this was Dell's direct response advertising method: to get the Dell product catalog, customers had to complete a detailed response card or call a toll-free number where they were asked the same, detailed questions. The Dell phone representatives were highly skilled, trained to ask questions and to listen to customers, recording their preferences and requirements in detail, and then acting on them.

Dell's approach highlights the need to develop the relationship with the customer.

In practice

Adopt a singular focus on the customer by following four principles.

1. *Finding the most efficient path to the customer*. This means avoiding intermediaries that add confusion and cost. Also, organize your business around customers who share similar needs.

2. *Making things easy – and being accountable*. Customers want fast, streamlined access to your products: give them this, and give them someone who will take responsibility for helping them.

3. *Building to order* – this means understanding what your customers want, and delivering exactly this. The result is less cost for you, and potentially more business from your client.

4. *Being a low-cost leader*. By focusing on what customers want, your business is able to reduce expensive inventory costs and to streamline your supply chain. The result is improved customer service, a better price for the customer, and higher margins for you.

IDEA 70
Age-sensitive management

Understanding the traits and desires of the different age groups present in the workplace will allow you to provide them with the incentives and motivation they truly value, improving overall corporate performance and morale.

The idea

Tesco, one of the UK's most successful retailers, employs people of different age groups so that their workforce is more representative of society as a whole. This enables Tesco to relate well to all its customers, who have a wide range of ages.

The contemporary workplace contains four age groups:

- silent veterans over 59 years old
- baby boomers aged 41–58
- Generation Xers aged 24–40.
- Generation Y aged 23 years and under.

Age-sensitive management suggests that these different groups have different expectations, and therefore require different management techniques and performance-based incentives.

Although it is not foolproof, it can provide a general guide to possible differences in the expectations of young and old employees. With an aging workforce and shifting demographics, the manager who can motivate regardless of age has a significant advantage.

In practice

The value of age-sensitive management is that employees are more motivated and customers are better served. The key is certainly not to discriminate on the basis of age, but rather to be sensitive to the attitudes of all your employees. What one group favors may not encourage or motivate another group of people of a different age.

- *Silent veterans* tend to have the most traditional ideas of interaction, favoring formal contact and face-to-face meetings. They typically value recognition of their skills and abilities.

- When managing *baby boomers*, clearly define goals and break down the process into a series of individual targets. Place an emphasis on teamwork and motivational talks. Rewards should be public, with noticeable displays of recognition.

- Allow *Generation Xers* slightly more freedom to achieve their targets: tell them what to do, but allow them to decide how to achieve the goal. Keep channels of communication open to allow ideas, opinions, and feedback to be discussed in a candid and honest way. Practical rewards, such as days off or monetary bonuses, are welcomed.

- *Generation Y* should be given plenty of opportunities to build their skills and experience – view yourself as both an instructive guide and a boss. Find out their personal goals, and make broader company targets relevant to those individual goals. Communication should be informal and positive.

IDEA 71
Three-factor theory

Three-factor theory is based on the premise that workers have basic human needs that management can and should work to address. Creating an environment in which these needs are met results in enthusiastic employees.

The idea

During the last three decades of the twentieth century, US-based firm Sirota Consulting surveyed 237 organizations worldwide across a range of industries, providing more than 2 million responses, about what employees wanted at work. This research suggests that there are three primary sets of goals for people at work (this is known as "three-factor theory"): equity, achievement, and camaraderie. For most workers, no other goals are nearly as important. Also, these goals have not changed in recent times, and cut across demographic groups and cultures. Establishing policies and practices in tune with these goals is, Sirota believes, the key to employee engagement.

In practice

Meeting the goals of equity, achievement, and camaraderie is the key to high morale and engagement, and is a condition for long-term success. The extent to which these three factors hold true for everyone is less important than the fact that they matter a great deal to many people.

Equity. This means being treated justly in relation to the basic conditions of employment. These basic conditions are:

- Physiological – such as having a safe working environment or manageable workload.

- Economic – including pay, benefits, and job security.

- Psychological – being treated consistently, fairly, considerately, and with respect.

Feelings of equity are influenced by a sense of relative treatment. For example, people ask themselves, am I being treated fairly in relation to my peers and colleagues?

Achievement. This means taking pride in one's accomplishments by doing things that matter and by doing them well, receiving recognition for those accomplishments, and taking pride in the team's accomplishments. Sirota Consulting's research suggests that this sense of achievement has six primary sources:

- the challenge of the work and the extent to which an employee can apply his/her skills and abilities

- acquiring new skills and the opportunity to develop, take risks, and expand personal horizons

- ability to perform – and possessing the resources, authority, information, and support to do the job well

- perceived importance of the job – knowing the work has a purpose and value, whether to the organization, customer, or society as a whole

- recognition for performance – this is non-financial as well as financial

- pride in the organization – resulting from the firm's purpose, success, ethics, the quality of its leadership, as well as the quality and impact of its products.

Camaraderie. Employees like to have warm, interesting, and cooperative relations with others in the workplace. The most significant aspects of camaraderie are:

- relationships with coworkers
- teamwork within a worker's business unit
- teamwork across departments in a specific location
- teamwork and cooperation across the entire organization.

Equity is the most important factor in shaping employee engagement. When equity is rated low, even if achievement and camaraderie are rated high, overall enthusiasm can be two-thirds lower.

Employee morale is a function of the way an organization is led, and the way that leadership is translated into daily management practices. Employee enthusiasm results in significant competitive advantage, as it impacts on all aspects of business success, including customer satisfaction. Finally, success breeds success, as morale drives performance and performance enhances morale in a virtuous cycle.

IDEA 72
Developing Islamic products

The Muslim population is growing fast, 1.2 billion and rising. Other religions are also gaining followers, and all are characterized by a commitment to faith-based principles. Recognizing that commerce can have a respectable, positive, and valuable role supporting people of faith is increasingly significant.

The idea

In common with most religious groups, Muslims have specific needs. Meeting these needs in the complex, fast-moving world of the early twenty-first century is a challenge, but also a significant opportunity.

For example, Takaful is as an alternative to conventional insurance that is compliant with Islamic (Shariah) law. From the Shariah perspective it is needed because although conventional insurance exists to protect customers, the way it operates poses problems. Several elements make it *haram* (not permissible) for Muslims to purchase insurance. These include: *gharar* (uncertainties), *maysir* (gambling), and *riba* or usury (interest).

Gharar is defined as any element in a contract that could lead to injustice or exploitation. It has a range of negative connotations encompassing uncertainty, deception, ambiguity, or ignorance. Muslim scholars believe that *gharar* exists in conventional insurance, because the benefits of protection that the plan offers are always uncertain: whether the benefits are deliverable depends on whether the insured event occurs or not.

In conventional insurance, Muslim jurists believe that the existence of *gharar* (uncertainties) leads to *maysir* (gambling). The gamble is that the insured may either lose all the premiums they have paid, or be compensated for losses incurred should the insured event occur. Gambling takes place whether the insured event occurs or not. This is because if the insured event occurs, policyholders will gain for being compensated for the loss they incur; however, if the insured event does not occur, the insurer will gain by keeping all the premiums that have been paid by the policyholders.

Riba (interest) is most prevalent in the investments of insurance funds. From the Shariah perspective, accumulation of wealth must always be free of interest. Therefore, the investments of insurance funds in interest-bearing securities such as bonds and stocks, which do not comply with Shariah principles, pose a major problem for Muslims purchasing conventional insurance.

SABB Takaful is an Islamic insurance business based in Saudi Arabia that is partly owned by the Saudi British Bank (SABB). Takaful means "guaranteeing each other" in Arabic. It is an Islamic system of mutual insurance built around the concept of *tabarru* (donation or gift). *Tabarru* contributions are made with the intention of helping other participants faced with difficulties. This eliminates the resemblance of Takaful to gambling and exploitation. Each participant contributes to a fund to cover expected claims, while also benefiting from a share of investment returns.

SABB Takaful manages their operations and invests contributions in line with the principles of Shariah. Participants share in the profits of the fund with the understanding that these may be forfeited to cover losses. When there is surplus, it is jointly shared. With Takaful, contributions are pooled into one fund that will be used to pay for any contingency should any of the scheme's members suffer a catastrophic loss. In other words, by guaranteeing compensation from the Takaful fund for the defined losses incurred by any members of the scheme, all the members of the scheme essentially protect each other.

In practice

Takaful insurance is growing rapidly in the Muslim world, as financial service firms recognize that sound financial management and religion are compatible, and possibly even complementary. Although it only launched in 2007, the future for SABB Takaful – a well-run, ethical business – is promising. The question is, why is it taking so long for firms to realize the opportunities here? Businesses not only make a profit but help people in a positive, socially responsible way as well – by supporting their personal faith.

One question that is increasingly significant, and I suspect unusual, is how can your business support people of faith?

IDEA 73
Support and challenge groups

One of the simplest, shortest, and most effective business ideas is to encourage people to establish support and challenge groups. Practiced by many organizations worldwide, these are an indispensable way to build teamwork, productivity, and effectiveness at work.

The idea

A support and challenge group consists of four or five colleagues of a similar level or status, who meet, informally, at regular intervals (perhaps once a month or once a week). Each individual takes a turn for ten minutes or so explaining a challenge or issue that they face. The others listen and then ask questions, helping their colleague understand the key issues and where the solution might lie. This should be done without prescribing a solution; the key is to support the individual and challenge their thinking and assumptions.

The UK retail pharmacist chain Boots is among many that have used the technique successfully. Support and challenge groups work for several reasons:

- Speaking about an issue or challenge can help provide perspective and clarify the issues, even without the comments of colleagues.

- The views of others can provide a different approach to a challenge – or simply provide encouragement and strength. Either way, the involvement of others is helpful.

- People gain greater understanding of each issue and the challenges they face. Being aware of common issues encourages people to collaborate more.

- Listening to someone else's challenge enables individuals to sharpen their own thinking and approach.

In practice

- Gather together a group of colleagues, explain the concept (to provide support and challenge each other's thinking), and arrange to meet regularly.

- One person keeps time – a speaker should take no more than ten minutes to explain their challenge.

- Ensure that the speaker is heard in silence, without interruption.

- Take it in turns to ask questions and comment. A questioning approach is particularly effective.

- Move on to the next individual and repeat the process.

IDEA 74
Clear strategy

Developing strategy is often over-elaborate and over-complicated. Strategy is simply about understanding where you are now, where you are heading, and how you will get there. It involves tough choices in three areas: who to target as customers, what products to offer, and how to implement the strategy efficiently. The most common cause of failure is the inability to make clear choices in these three areas.

The idea

The importance of making clear choices in the three elements of strategy – who to target, what to offer, and how best to implement – is best shown by the example of Nespresso, a simple-to-use espresso machine developed by the Swiss giant Nestlé. Though it is simple in appearance and use, Nestlé spent more than ten years developing it.

After several years of limited success, a new strategy improved profitability. The system consists of two parts: a coffee capsule and a machine. The coffee side of the operation was separated from the machine side, with the machines being made and sold by other companies. Nestlé was no longer responsible for the sales or maintenance of the machines – which was not its area of expertise – but, crucially, the machines could only use Nespresso capsules, guaranteeing future sales of coffee. The target customer was changed from offices to households, and the sales process was managed exclusively through the

Nespresso Club (by phone, fax, or website, with capsules shipped direct to the customer).

In practice

To ensure a successful strategy:

1. *Create a unique strategic position for your company.* Focus on who your customers are, the value proposition offered to customers, and how you can do this efficiently. (Do not confuse strategy with vision, mission, or objectives.)

2. *Make distinctive and meaningful choices.* Combine these choices in a self-reinforcing system of activities that fit together. Common mistakes include keeping options open, enabling people to ignore choices, an approach to achieving growth that forces people to ignore the firm's overarching strategy, and analysis paralysis.

3. *Understand the importance of values and incentives.* The culture and values, measurement and incentives, people, structure, and processes all determine the environment of your organization. By influencing behavior, these will affect the success of your strategy.

4. *Gain people's emotional commitment to the strategy.* Any strategy will fail unless people are emotionally committed to its success.

5. *Recognize that understanding is not the same as communicating.* Explain why the strategy is important to the organization and the individual.

6. *Do not overlook the knowing–doing gap.* Individuals tend to do the urgent things and not the important ones.

7. *Do not assume that strategy can only be developed by "top" people.* Ideas can come from anybody, anytime, anywhere.

8. *Keep your strategy flexible.* Ideas have a shelf life. Continually

reassess the answers to the "who, what, and how" questions. Also, strategy requires adjustment to suit external circumstances. So allow your people to respond and to adjust, without waiting for permission.

In every industry, there are several positions that a company can occupy. The essence of strategy is to choose the one position that your company will claim as its own. If this is achieved, the firm can stake out a unique strategic position.

IDEA 75
Six-hat thinking

"Six thinking hats" is a powerful technique created by Edward de Bono. It is used to look at decisions from a number of perspectives, helping you to think differently and acquire a rounded view of a situation.

The idea

Many successful people think from a rational, positive viewpoint. However, if they do not look at a problem from an emotional, creative, or negative viewpoint, they can underestimate resistance to plans, fail to make creative leaps, and overlook the importance of contingency plans. Conversely, pessimists can be excessively defensive, while emotional people can fail to look at decisions calmly and rationally. Each of these "thinking hats" is a different style of thinking, and the "six thinking hats" technique will help you assess problems from many angles, enabling decisions to combine ambition, effectiveness, sensitivity, and creativity.

In practice

Adopt a different hat based on your situation and priorities.

1. *White hat*. Focus on the data available. Look at the information you have and see what you can learn from it. Look for gaps in your knowledge and either try to fill them or take account of them, by analyzing past trends and extrapolating from data.

2. *Red hat*. Look at problems using intuition, gut reaction, and emotion. Try to think how other people will react emotionally, and try to understand the responses of people who do not know your reasoning.

3. *Black hat*. Look at all the bad points of the issue, trying to see why it might not work. This highlights the weak points in a plan, allowing you to eliminate or alter them or to prepare contingency plans for them. This helps to make plans more resilient. It is one of the real benefits of this technique, as problems can be anticipated and countered.

4. *Yellow hat*. This requires thinking positively and optimistically, helping you to see the benefits of the decision. It helps you to keep going when everything looks difficult.

5. *Green hat*. This involves developing creative solutions. It is a freewheeling way of thinking, in which there is little criticism of ideas.

6. *Blue hat*. This emphasizes process control, and is exhibited by people chairing meetings. When ideas are running dry, it can be useful to use green-hat thinking, as the creative approach can stimulate fresh ideas.

IDEA 76
Building business relationships

By giving greater priority to the quality of relationships internally with colleagues and externally with customers and others, businesses will prosper.

The idea

Leaders often claim that "people are our greatest asset" – without any real understanding of what this means in practice. Optima is a business based in London that helps individuals to improve leadership skills, and organizations to improve the way they do business. Optima's focus (and main source of differentiation) is helping to build "amazing business relationships." Optima's success highlights the value and appeal of its approach. More than that, it is widely regarded as a great place to work and do business.

Building business relationships is an obvious yet difficult task to achieve, requiring productive, open, supportive, and assertive relationships, both inside and outside the organization. If people are an organization's greatest asset, it is sensible to focus on getting the most from that asset through productive, positive relationships.

In practice

How can you develop trusted business relationships? Most of us are taught the answer when we are children, we just seem to forget the essentials as we grow older. Several simple rules can help you get started:

- *Display genuine warmth.* Be supportive, open, positive, empathic, constructive, and engaging – not simply "friendly."

- *Be confident.* Be challenging, in control, confident, strong, authoritative, and direct.

- *Display assertive behavior.* Combine appropriate levels of challenge and support.

- *Listen.* Be open and genuine, and listen in a way that seeks mutual benefit.

- *Build trust.* Be diligent and consistent, acting with integrity and sincerity:

  - Deliver what you say you will and treat others as you would wish to be treated.
  - Understand who you are dealing with; take time to find out how others work and what motivates them.
  - Understand and trust yourself. Self-trust is essential to creating positive relationships.
  - Show commitment and value reciprocal relationships. Trust requires commitment, personal responsibility, and vigilance.
  - Consider why people should (or do) respect you. Understand your own motivation and objectives.
  - Remember that trust is time-sensitive and fragile – it takes time and attention to develop.
  - Be clear and honest – without hidden agendas.
  - Show your passion.

IDEA 77
Learning together

Responding to changes in business markets is best achieved with a willingness to learn and develop ideas as part of a group, creating an 'intensive learning culture'.

The idea

Nokia, the world-renowned mobile telephony company was, in the late 1980s, a nearly defunct diversified conglomerate, mostly known for its rubber and tissue products. The decision to put all the energy and remaining resources behind a minuscule (by industry standards) telecommunications activity, more specifically an emerging mobile telephony sector, triggered an intensive learning culture and period of business growth.

By the end of 1996 Nokia Group was the global market leader in digital mobile phones, and one of the two largest suppliers of GSM networks. In just a few years, this resilient Finnish business had learned enough to become the trendsetter in mobile phone design, making their product a high-tech lifestyle attribute that many fashion products could envy. On the mobile network side, Nokia was also setting the pace with solution-oriented customer services, thus raising the competitive threshold.

Most companies, having achieved this level of success in such a short time, could be expected to miss the next industry turn if there ever was one – and there was: the rise of the Internet. However, Nokia kept pace with this change, creating phones that were internet-ready, and helped create the now ubiquitous mobile information culture.

Commenting on Nokia's "thinking process" CEO Jorma Ollila noted:

> Of course, we get masses of information, but what is important is that we discuss it a lot among ourselves, kicking it around, looking at it from different perspectives. It is a collective learning process and the key point is whom we should discuss a new piece of information with, to augment it and give it more meaning than it had originally. Then, we make some choices, try them out, listen to the feedback and redirect as needed. With this collective learning process we are all on the same wavelength and we can act very fast when needed.

Nokia has certainly suffered its share of setbacks, but to successfully make a journey from near disaster to world domination in less than ten years shows a sustained flexibility and desire to learn at all levels. Clearly this is vital for a business in an industry as new and fast moving as mobile telephony, but the Nokia approach – applied throughout a business – highlights the value of moving from information to knowledge.

In practice

- Capture, disseminate, share, analyze and discuss information and insights.

- Hold regular discussion groups consisting of people working at all levels inside the company as well as external experts.

- Discuss the significance of developments in the market, as well as possible future trends and scenarios.

- If it is decided that the company should bring in new policies or move in a different direction, then brainstorm the workability and practicality of these changes. Decide who will implement them, and how.

IDEA 78
Microfinance

Microfinance is the business of lending small sums of money to entrepreneurs in the developing world, recognizing the ingenuity and commercialism of some of the world's poor.

The idea

Microfinance works by loaning customers relatively small amounts of capital (e.g. $50) at a commercial rate of interest. This leads to the development of a product or to the realization of an idea. This loan is typically made via a local bank – a group of people who administer the scheme. This lending process stimulates a self-sustaining cycle of wealth creation.

Initially, major banks and financial service institutions, as well as governments and NGOs, were skeptical. Times have changed, and many organizations can now see the commercial, economic, and humanitarian value of this activity. FINCA International has supported this work and, together with others (such as Grameen Bank in Bangladesh), has shown that microcredit works well. In the view of Rupert Scofield, executive director of FINCA: "My hope is that this type of programme encourages people to be honest, treat each other with respect and succeed. What really matters is how determined people are to succeed."

Founded in 1984, FINCA (the Foundation for International Community Assistance) is a non-profit agency that pioneered microfinance – or "village banking."

In practice

By addressing humanitarian concerns, microfinance provides hope and promotes prosperity. In encouraging responsibility and generating greater participation in society, it delivers other benefits, such as greater political, social, and economic stability.

IDEA 79
Surviving a downturn

Several clear principles and techniques can help turn a business round from the brink of disaster.

The idea

By the end of 1999, significant problems emerged at US technology giant Xerox. There was too much change, too fast; new, opportunistic competitors emerged; economic growth was slowing; key decisions were flawed. These issues combined with regulatory and liquidity challenges to bring about a massive decline in revenues, the departure of customers and employees, and debts of US$19 billion.

Despite this, Xerox, led by CEO Anne Mulcahy, survived the downturn and staged a remarkable comeback. The business had doubled its share price by 2006, reduced costs by US$2 billion, and achieved profits of US$1 billion in 2005.

The foundation for a revival in Xerox came from a strong brand with a loyal customer base, talented employees, recognition of the need to listen carefully to customers, and greater responsiveness. The key was to win back market share with a competitive range of new products.

In practice

Several factors underpinned Xerox's resurgence, outlining the key areas to address:

- Listen to customers, employees, and people who know the business. Create a culture of good critics, and be aware that managers can become out of touch, even within their own organization.

- Learn Six Sigma – it can improve costs and service for customers, by providing a disciplined way to make process improvements.

- Recognize the need to be "problem curious," constantly looking for ways to differentiate and improve.

- Provide a clear, exciting, compelling vision of what the future will look like. People value a guiding light, as it provides certainty.

- Invest in the future and innovate. In 2005, two-thirds of Xerox's revenues came from products launched within the previous two years.

- Be entrepreneurial – find ways to sell products and control costs.

- Manage cash.

- Remember that strong leadership is essential. A business relies on its people – and people need to be aligned around a common set of goals and plans.

IDEA 80
Innovation culture

Encouraging people in your organization to see things differently attracts the best employees and increases the distinctiveness and value of your business.

The idea

A UK-based innovation company, ?What If!, shows clients how to make their organizations more innovative. Their processes challenge people to see things differently by stepping out of their comfort zones and risking ideas that may seem to make little sense. Two key, but separate, processes are needed for innovation:

- idea building, where people propose ideas and then develop and nurture them

- idea analysis, where these ideas are assessed.

Companies that struggle to be innovative often do so because ideas get stifled in their infancy by an excessive rush to judgment and analysis.

Having the right kind of processes for idea generation and innovation is important, but processes are not enough. Innovative organizations also have a general environment and culture that values and fosters innovation.

In practice

Research by the Talent Foundation identified five catalysts for successful innovation:

1. *Consciousness*. Each person knows the goals of the organization and believes they can play a part in achieving them.

2. *Multiplicity*. Teams and groups contain a wide and creative mix of skills, experiences, backgrounds, and ideas.

3. *Connectivity*. Relationships are strong and trusting, and are actively encouraged and supported within and across teams and functions.

4. *Accessibility*. Doors and minds are open; everyone in the organization has access to resources, time, and decision makers.

5. *Consistency*. Commitment to innovation runs throughout the organization and is built into processes and leadership style.

IDEA 81
Resource building

The key to success lies in viewing the essentials of business (such as people, customers, cash, ideas, skills, reputation, and others) as resources that accumulate or decline. By taking a resource-based view you will make decisions that are dynamic and forward-focused, rather than historically based.

The idea

Resources interact and interconnect. This simple fact holds the key to growing and developing a business, as plans and decisions are more likely to succeed.

In *The Critical Path* and *Competitive Strategy Dynamics*, Professor Kim Warren of London Business School explains that the greatest challenge facing managers is understanding and driving performance into the future. "When the causes of performance through time are not understood, companies tend to make poor choices about their future … . The "critical path" is the journey the business takes as it builds resources and tackles the strategic challenge of developing future performance."

Japanese technology firm Canon recognized the importance of resource building in the 1970s. To overcome the formidable advantages of Xerox, the market leader, Canon focused on building tangible and direct resources (such as customers, products, distributors, and cash) and intangible, indirect resources (such as brand reputation). Canon designed copiers for maximum reliability, made replacement parts modular so that end-use customers could replace them, and ensured designs were so simple that dealers could be trained to make repairs. Canon's approach meant Xerox failed to sustain its competitive advantage.

Business success is determined by whether resources strengthen or decline, complement or undermine each other, take from or are eroded by competitors.

In practice

Three basic issues need to be addressed: why performance is following its current path, where current policies and strategy will lead, and how the future can be altered for the better. Several steps will help address these issues:

1. Identify resources and understand how they behave. You do not have to possess a resource for it to be useful. Consider the following questions:

   - What are the most significant resources in your organization?
   - How many of these resources do you have?
   - How do they interact and affect each other? In particular, how do they affect the quantity and quality of other resources?

2. Consider the impact that people have on this system:

   - Do you use people to build, develop, retain, and use resources?
   - Do you ensure that people enhance the quality of your resources?

3. Understand how resources affect performance.

4. Develop new resources in your business.

5. Recognize the outside forces driving resource flows.

6. Understand and leverage interdependence between resources.

7. Upgrade your resources. Check you are not approaching any quality problems, by identifying resources in danger of running out, declining in quality, or having the potential to damage other resources.

IDEA 82
Building trust

Trust is an essential aspect of business, notably when leading people, selling to customers, or building the long-term reputation and value of an enterprise. Trust is easily taken for granted, hard to define, and easy to undermine or destroy – but how can it be built?

The idea

Trust matters in business, underpinning issues as diverse as sales, financial management, and leadership, as well as affecting job satisfaction and career prospects. However, increased profitability is not the most compelling reason to build trust. People value trust, but what is overlooked is that its absence results not in a neutral situation but in something worse. As businesses have discovered, when trust is undermined there is a high cost to pay.

The Innocent Drinks Company epitomizes many of the characteristics of a high-trust organization. It produces high-quality fruit drinks and smoothies with a passion, professionalism, and good humor that invite trust. This tone is set from the top. Like many trusted leaders, the executives at Innocent Drinks do not spend much time focusing on trust. Instead, they simply display the energy and skills that people (employees and customers) value – and trust follows. This avoids the paradox of trust, where the more it is discussed, the weaker it becomes.

In practice

In recent research, people were asked to rate the significance of a range of attributes when deciding whether to trust someone. The most popular attributes are fairness, dependability, respect, openness, courage, unselfishness, competence, supportiveness, empathy, compassion, and passion. These drivers of trust need to be understood and delivered, if trust is to be developed.

There are several practical steps to developing trust, but the most fundamental one is to be genuine: you have to mean what you say and be sincere in your approach. Consider the following actions:

- Deliver what you say you will, and be true to your word.

- Create an atmosphere and expectation of trust by trusting others.

- Keep team members informed by asking what information would be most helpful, explaining issues carefully, and sharing available information.

- Give constructive feedback by clearly identifying the behavior that you are giving feedback on (focus on the behavior, not the person).

- Act with integrity and sincerity.

- Treat others as you would wish to be treated yourself.

- Understand who you are dealing with, taking time to find out how they work and what motivates them.

- Be dutiful, diligent, and consistent.

- Recognize success and reward good performance.

IDEA 83
Emotional intelligence

Emotional intelligence (EI) is a person's ability to acquire and apply knowledge from their emotions and the emotions of others, in order to be more successful and lead a more fulfilling life.

The idea

Psychologist Daniel Goleman popularized his view of emotional intelligence in the 1995 best-seller *Emotional Intelligence: Why it can matter more than IQ*. Building on the work of Howard Gardner and Peter Salovey, he highlighted the fact that EI is evident in five key areas:

- knowing one's emotions
- managing emotions
- motivating oneself
- recognizing emotions in others
- handling relationships.

Emotions are critical in determining a leader's success. In times of change, pressure, or crisis, possessing EI is advantageous, as success is determined by recognizing, understanding, and dealing with emotions. For example, we may all feel anger, but EI means knowing what to do with the emotion of anger to achieve the best outcome. EI enables us to sense and use emotions, helping us to manage ourselves and influence positive outcomes in our relationships.

In practice

EI can be learnt. Succeeding with EI is achieved by heightening ability in the following areas:

1. *Self-awareness*. Despite the fact that our moods run alongside our thoughts, we rarely pay much attention to the way we feel. This is significant because previous emotional experiences provide a context for our decision making.

2. *Managing emotions*. All effective leaders learn to manage their emotions, especially the big three emotions: anger, anxiety, and sadness.

3. *Motivating others*. Motivating involves creating a supportive, enthusiastic environment, being sensitive to the issues that increase or reduce the enthusiasm of each individual, and providing the right approach to move and guide people in the right direction.

4. *Showing empathy*. The flip side of self-awareness is the ability to correctly understand, and adjust to, emotions in others.

5. *Staying connected*. Emotions are contagious: there is an unseen transaction that passes between individuals in every interaction, making us feel either a little better or a little worse. Goleman refers to this as a "secret economy," and it holds the key to motivating people.

These "emotional competencies" build on each other in a hierarchy. At the bottom of Goleman's hierarchy (1) is the ability to identity one's emotional state. Some knowledge of competency

1 is needed to move to the next competency. Likewise, knowledge or skill in the first three competencies is needed to show empathy, reading and influencing positively other people's emotions (competency 4). The first four competencies lead to increased ability to enter and sustain good relationships (competency 5).

IDEA 84
The balanced scorecard

In *The Balanced Scorecard* Robert Kaplan and David Norton highlight several ways entrepreneurs can increase the long-term value of their business. The balanced scorecard offers a measurement and management system that links strategic objectives to improved performance.

The idea

The balanced scorecard approach enables managers to generate objectives in four business areas, providing a framework for action, with progress being regularly assessed. Its success lies in its ability to unify and integrate a set of indicators that measure the performance of key activities and processes at the core of the organization's operations. This presents a balanced picture, and highlights specific activities that need to be completed.

The balanced scorecard takes into account four essential areas – traditional "hard" financial measures are only one part. The three "soft," quantifiable operational measures include:

- customer perspective – how an organization is perceived by customers

- internal perspective – those issues in which the organization must excel

- innovation and learning perspective – those areas where an organization must continue to improve and add value.

Two of the highest-profile and most successful examples of the balanced scorecard at work are provided by Mobil Oil (now Exxon Mobil) and Cigna Insurance. Exxon moved from last to first in profitability within its industry from 1993 to 1995 – a position it maintained for four years. Cigna Insurance was losing $1 million a day in 1993, but within two years it was in the top quartile of profitability in its industry. Both organizations attribute a significant element of their success to the balanced scorecard.

In practice

The type, size, and structure of an organization will determine the detail of the implementation process. However, the main stages involved include:

1. *Preparing and defining the strategy*. The first requirement is to clearly define and communicate the strategy, ensuring that people have an understanding of the strategic objectives or goals, and the three or four critical success factors that are fundamental to achieving each objective or goal.

2. *Deciding what to measure*. Goals and measures should be determined for each of the four perspectives: financial, customers, internal processes, and innovation and learning perspective. Examples for each are included overleaf.

3. *Finalizing and implementing the plan*. Further discussions are necessary to agree the detail of the goals and activities to be measured, and what precise measures should be used. This is the real value in the approach: deciding what action to take to achieve the goal.

4. *Communicating and implementing*. Delegate balanced scorecards throughout the organization.

Perspective	Goals	Measures
Financial	■ Increased profitability ■ Share price performance ■ Increased return on assets	■ Cash-flows ■ Cost reduction ■ Gross margins ■ Return on capital / equity / investments / sales ■ Revenue growth ■ Payment terms
Customers	■ New customer acquisition ■ Customer retention ■ Customer satisfaction ■ Cross-sales volumes	■ Market share ■ Customer service and satisfaction ■ Number of complaints ■ Customer profitability ■ Delivery times ■ Units sold ■ Number of customers
Internal processes	■ Improved core competencies ■ Improved critical technologies ■ Streamlined processes ■ Improved employee morale	■ Efficiency improvements ■ Improved lead times ■ Reduced unit costs ■ Reduced waste ■ Improved sourcing / supplier delivery ■ Greater employee morale and satisfaction, and reduced staff turnover ■ Internal audit standards ■ Sales per employee
Innovation and learning perspective	■ New product development ■ Continuous improvement ■ Employees' training and skills	■ Number of new products ■ Sales of new products ■ Number of employees receiving training ■ Outputs from employees' training ■ Training hours per employee ■ Number and scope of skills learned

Diagram: the balanced scorecard

5. *Publicizing and using the results.* While everyone should understand the overall objectives, deciding who should receive specific information, why and how often, is also important. Too much detail can lead to paralysis by analysis; too little, and the benefits are lost. Use the information to guide decisions, strengthening areas that need further action, and using the process dynamically.

6. *Reviewing and revising the system.* This allows wrinkles to be smoothed out and new challenges to be set. The best way to tell whether the balanced scorecard is working for your business is to set higher measurement goals every year, and continue to meet them.

IDEA 85
Developing a sales culture

"Putting customers first" is a frequently heard business mantra, but what does it mean and how can it be achieved in practice?

The idea

The argument is simple. If you can get everyone in your organization to view their work from the point of the view the consumer, your business will be more effective and likely to succeed. This sounds obvious but can be hard to achieve. The challenge is to overcome the inertia of previous attitudes and to instill a new sense of energy and a focus on the customer.

In practice

HSBC is a financial services business that since 1992 has achieved a compound annual growth rate of 17 percent. It has become one of the world's ten largest corporations, and since 2004 has been striving to achieve organic growth, largely by focusing on current and potential customers (rather than through acquisitions or improving business processes). Shifting the approach of a large, venerable, and long-standing bank that employs over 300,000 people in 80 countries is no mean feat. Several factors are prominent in its move to a greater sales focus:

- *Proactively manage performance*. Get the right people working at their best, and make sure everyone knows that success is determined by the customer. Help individuals to achieve their potential; if you need to change the people you have in the business, do so.

- *Ensure you have the right management information*. It informs decision making and shows people the indicators and issues that they need to focus on.

- *Establish a robust sales process*. This will ensure the basics are being covered, while emphasizing what matters and providing a framework for action.

- *Value relationships*. Relationship management is central to a sales culture because it leads to greater understanding of customers. Thinking of customers in terms of your relationship together takes them from being a statistic to being something that is more significant and valuable.

- *Segment your customers*. This leads to greater clarity, insight, and success. This is important in competitive, fast-moving markets, and ensures offers are more likely to appeal because they are matched with the right customers.

- *Avoid complacency and develop an entrepreneurial approach*. This is hard to achieve because it relies on the other stages being accomplished first. With the other measures in place, the culture and focus of the business will inevitably change and strengthen.

- *Display strong leadership*. This includes the need to communicate, to act as a role model for the values that you believe are important, to inspire trust, and to be personally effective.

IDEA 86
Market segmentation

Market segmentation involves analyzing groups of current and potential customers. It is valuable for understanding the organization and composition of the market, to improve the effectiveness of marketing plans, and to target potential customers.

The idea

A senior marketing colleague once remarked that he wanted to see "all of our customers broken down by age and sex," until I pointed out that most of them were already. What he meant was he wanted to better understand our customers: who they are and what they valued. This enabled him to match products with customers, as well as informing his thinking about many other issues: from new product development to pricing and distribution. This is the challenge of segmentation.

Many industries and businesses are improving their market segmentation, for example, by using psychographic profiling that divides customers into "groups" according to personal needs, preferences, and lifestyle. Some of the best segmenters are financial service businesses, such as credit card companies, insurers, and banks. The business of lending money is difficult: match the wrong loan or product to the wrong people, and either you miss a sale or they default. There is a vital need to target the right people from the start. This has the great benefit of increasing marketing efficiency.

In practice

- Segmentation needs to be focused: the larger a segment, the greater the danger that it will lose value.

- The key to segmentation lies in highlighting differences and specific characteristics: this requires clarity and insight.

- Segmentation should be as simple as possible, avoiding unnecessary complications and ensuring decisions and views are rational and clearly communicated.

- Segmentation needs certainty. It is tempting to jump to conclusions or make assumptions about segments based on your own experience, background, or prejudice. However, these can be mistaken and a key element in successful segmentation is analysis: understanding how something is, and why it is that way.

IDEA 87
Audacity

How do you instill a bold, adventurous approach in employees? The most successful businesses are often those that are prepared to go further and take careful, calculated risks. This spirit of audacity can be developed, with insightful leadership.

The idea

"As South Africans, we weren't really frightened of emerging markets compared to the things that we were going through at home," commented Graham Mackay, SABMiller's chief executive. Difficult trading and environmental conditions instilled determination and resilience in managers at SABMiller, one of the world's largest brewers. Having built SAB in their domestic market, they were keen to compete and succeed abroad following the end of apartheid. They were ingenious, flexible, determined, and prepared not to follow convention. For example, SAB entered markets that (from the mid-1990s) were unfashionable, in Latin America, China, and Central Europe. Although these developing economies represent attractive growth markets now, the fact that SAB had a culture of taking on challenges meant that it could go there first and achieve considerable success.

SABMiller has a bold approach to business and has become a global giant in little over ten years.

In practice

- *Find the dangerous edge.* This is the point where the greatest risks lie. Understanding where this point is will increase confidence and your ability to avoid disaster. This enables you to understand what you do not know.

- *Be supportive.* This means building a supportive environment and being specific about what will happen in any situation. Start by accepting and explaining the risk, but finish by emphasizing strengths and visualizing success.

- *Build a confidence frame.* Gradually build confidence in steady increments.

- *Develop ancillary skills.* Being good at a wide range of relevant tasks will help build confidence, especially in complex situations, and promote success.

- *Recognize that moving into a "danger zone" has positive psychological benefits.* These include heightened awareness and concentration.

IDEA 88
Silo busting

How do you get people to collaborate within an organization across business divisions? The answer is to focus on the thing that should unite you most – the need to serve customers – in five practical ways.

The idea

Many businesses have either failed or not realized their potential because they were divided by rivalry and did not adequately serve customers. This matters at any time, but is particularly problematic if the firm is launching a new product or looking to sell more to existing clients and contacts.

In 2001, GE Medical Systems (now GE Healthcare) started providing consultancy services (known as Performance Solutions) to complement its sales of imaging equipment. Initial sales for consultancy services were strong, but declined by 2005 because of a lack of coordination between divisions selling equipment and consultancy. Its response was to alter its approach, to be more customer-centered, and to change the sales organization.

In practice

- *Start by increasing coordination across boundaries*. This can be done in three ways: sharing information, especially about customers; sharing people and skills; and as far as possible, making collective decisions. The danger is that traditional silos will be replaced by customer-focused ones – yet even this is a step forward. The key is to overcome traditional divisions.

- *Implement new performance measures and metrics centered on customers.* Metrics encourage customer-focused decisions. If these metrics are linked with rewards, they can be a powerful way to change behavior.

- *Develop cooperation by changing the structure and approach of specific teams.* This can be challenging, and may include changing reporting arrangements and revising processes so that people closest to the customers are the ones making more of the key decisions.

- *Build cross-business skills and capabilities.* Silo busting requires generalists, people capable of operating across divisions. These people should be developed and programs implemented to help them gain and develop their cross-business expertise.

- *Build relationships and connect with people.* There is no substitute for the "soft" skills of rapport, understanding, and trust. Involvement, communication, and support are valuable ways to build relationships, and these will help ensure success.

IDEA 89
Selling online

Selling online is a fast, flexible, and highly effective way to reach customers and increase revenues. Online sales are growing at a phenomenally fast rate – and yet the first online sale occurred as recently as 1994 in the USA. What are the lessons, and how can a business increase online sales?

The idea

Meeting the challenges of selling online and integrating online activities with the whole business is essential for success. Seven basic principles characterize online selling:

1. The balance of power is continuing to shift decisively to the customer.

2. The internet is revolutionizing sales techniques and perceptions of leading brands.

3. The pace of business activity and change has been accelerating, and the need to be flexible, adaptive, customer-focused, and innovative is at a premium.

4. Competition is intensifying.

5. Managing and leveraging knowledge is fundamental – knowledge is a key strategic resource that needs to be captured, nurtured, and developed.

6. Companies are transforming themselves into extended

enterprises to add value for customers. They are re-evaluating factors as fundamental as objectives, markets, and skills.

7. The internet is increasing interactivity among people, companies, and industries.

Online selling is immediate, and enables businesses to reduce costs, while improving marketing effectiveness. The Economist Intelligence Unit, an international publisher of business information and part of the Economist Group, has successfully developed an online business that is seamlessly integrated with its products and overall approach.

In practice

Several fundamental steps will enhance online sales.

- Generate participation, ownership, and commitment within your business.

- Ensure that your internet selling strategy is all-embracing and dynamic, continually evolving, and learning from past experience.

- Simplify the customer's experience so that the sales process is streamlined, with barriers to purchasing removed.

- Ensure that your website is sticky and compelling. Customers need to remain at your website (known as "stickiness") – your competitor is only a click or two away – and you need to ensure that customers come back time and again.

- Focus on flexibility and personalization so that customers are empowered to buy exactly what they want, their way.

- Avoid duplication and a complicated, high-cost approach when an effective, low-cost alternative is available.

- Plan and prepare for the benefits of an internet sales strategy, so that you avoid investing too much, too little, too late, or too soon.

- Help customers (as well as distributors and sales people) to navigate easily through your site. Enable customers to move in a seamless flow, with simple decisions and preferences included in the process, so they can make decisions and express preferences during the process.

- Ensure that the website, or the web provider and developer, is flexible enough to take account of ways in which your website requirements may evolve.

- Ensure that your website is competitive: to achieve this it needs to provide an experience for the customer that is simple, interactive, engaging, and compelling.

- Give customers access to your information so that they can quickly and easily decide how best to buy. The advantage of this is that it can be a two-way process. It provides you with opportunities to capture and use specific information about each customer (data mining), as well as enabling you to enhance the effectiveness of your website, following the pattern and flow of customers' mouse clicks while online (clickstream data).

IDEA 90
Value innovation

When firms compete, they tend to become locked in a cycle of incrementally improving a combination of costs, product, and service. Value innovators break free from the pack by staking out a new market, developing products or services for which there are no direct competitors.

The idea

Pioneered by W. Chan Kim and Renée Mauborgne, value innovation is the concept of challenging and defying conventional logic to either redefine or create a market. For example, for many years, US TV networks used the same format for news programs: they aired at the same time, and they competed on the popularity and professionalism of their presenters and their ability to report and analyze events. This changed in 1980, when CNN launched real-time 24-hour news from around the world for only 20 percent of the cost of the networks.

Similarly, in 1984 Virgin defied convention when it decided to eliminate its first-class service. Prevailing logic suggested that growth relied on focusing on more, not fewer, market segments, but Virgin focused on business-class passengers. It used the money saved from first class to provide a range of popular innovations, from better and different lounges to improved in-flight amenities. This approach was later applied to its other businesses, such as retailing and music.

In practice

Underpinning value innovation is the ability to redefine a business strategy based on an understanding of customers.

- *Work at dramatically improving everything you offer the customer*: product, service, and delivery.

- *Challenge and overcome industry assumptions*. Understand what these assumptions are and how the situation can be improved for customers.

- *Adopt a questioning approach*. Why do customers buy? What would they really value? Why do they want this? How does this purchase relate to their other priorities?

- *Be ambitious*. Monitoring competitors is good, but avoid the trap of competing with them on their (or the industry's) terms. Concentrate on doing something different and valuable for the customer. Aim high, and competitive strength will follow.

- *Avoid segmentation*. While many people insist segmentation provides greater understanding of customers, enabling them to be served better, value innovators build scale by focusing on the features that unite customers. This is the key to profitability: appealing to sufficient numbers of people and achieving scale.

- *Do not be constrained by existing resources*. The question is not what you can do with current assets and capabilities, but what resources you should develop to serve your customers.

- *Think laterally*. This involves cutting across traditional industry divisions between product and service, and finding ways to significantly improve the offer to the customer.

IDEA 91
Talent
management

Whatever your business, having the right people in the right roles is essential for success. Talent management ensures that you have a steady supply of one of the scarcest, most expensive, and important resources: the right people.

The idea

Good people are hard to find, and during a time of relative economic prosperity and declining population, notably in developed Western countries, it is becoming harder and more competitive to find talented people. The solution is talent management: attracting, developing, and retaining the right people.

Nurturing, developing, and retaining the most talented people requires specific, in-depth skills and expertise. The importance of an explicit focus on talent management was evident in the experience of Mellon Financial, which developed through the 1990s from a traditional bank into a strong financial services business. The challenge was to develop new products and services, cross-sell to clients, and expand into new markets. This required new skills and a different approach, so Mellon, under CEO Marty McGuinn, took several important steps to manage talent within the organization. Centers of excellence were introduced, where experts devised leadership development tools and programs, which were taken into each business unit to provide training and development to individuals. The leadership development program involved senior management frequently meeting with emerging leaders one-to-one. The skills that emerging leaders would need were explained and individuals were helped to develop those skills. The focus on talent management was an important aspect of Mellon's development.

In practice

Addressing questions in several key areas will help you focus on talent management within your organization:

- *Corporate culture*. What are your priorities? Does your organization have the desired identity and culture? Do all of your employees understand your vision and core values? What keeps your employees coming to work each day? What affects their attitudes and behavior with your customers and with one another?

- *Recruitment and selection*. How do you identify and select the right people? Do you clearly understand the skills and experience required now and in the future, and do you get the best available people?

- *Managing performance*. Are you actively managing perform-ance, giving feedback, and coaching employees to improve?

- *Employee development*. Do you have adequate resources, processes, and tools to develop your employees? Do all employees have a personal development plan to improve their skills and maximize their potential?

- *Remuneration*. Are you properly rewarding your employees? Do your bonus schemes encourage and reward the desired behaviors?

- *Succession planning and leadership development.* Do you have succession plans for key roles?

- *Diversity, compliance, and procedures.* Does your workforce reflect the customers and markets you serve? Are you meeting your legal obligations? Are you engaging with key stakeholders and handling employee relations?

IDEA 92
The leadership pipeline

Make clear to everyone in your organization the skills they need to possess and the results they need to achieve if they are going to progress to the next level. This will help them succeed in their career, and boost your business along the way.

The idea

Many organizations only pay lip service to career planning. Yet, at a time when there is a shortage of the right people and skills, it really does pay to "grow your own" talent. One example of this working well is RBS Insurance, which makes clear to all of its employees:

- the skills that are needed at each level of management

- the skills that need to be developed before moving up to the next level

- the content of the role at each level and what it is that individuals do.

In their book *The Leadership Pipeline*, authors Ram Charan, Stephen Drotter and James Noel highlight six stages in the leadership journey: self-leadership, people, manager, unit (individuals responsible for the delivery of part of a business), business (individuals accountable for the results of a business), and enterprise leadership (individuals responsible for more than one business).

As individuals progress through the "leadership pipeline" they encounter different "transition challenges" – for example, moving into their first people-management role, when moving from self to people leadership. There is also a focus on specialist roles such as legal, accountancy, marketing, and finance.

The advantage of managing leadership transitions is that it provides a framework for leadership development, highlights what success looks like at each stage, and describes how to improve skills – from new employees to top executives. It also ensures consistency across the business, and above all, explains how to prepare for career advancement.

The leadership pipeline meets three business needs. It provides clarity about what is required, it makes the right development accessible for all, and it helps to focus development activities. Individuals benefit greatly from a clear, transparent career path.

In practice

- Identify the different stages or levels of leadership within your business.

- For each level, decide: a) what skills are required, b) what activities are involved and what leaders at that level actually do, c) how a leader needs to prepare for the next level – what skills and activities are missing that will be needed at the higher level?

- Provide practical processes and tools, such as personal development planning, coaching, and development programs to help make the transition.

IDEA 93
Hardball

Competing means striving to get ahead of the competition, but hardball goes further: it is about relentlessly developing and then sustaining a clear gap between you and your nearest rivals. It is highlighted in the article "Hardball Strategies" (*Harvard Business Review*, September 2006, by Lachenauer, R; MacMillan, Ian C.; van Putten, Alexander B.; Gunther McGrath, Rita; Stalk, George Jr.).

The idea

It is fashionable to think that playing tough is doomed to failure: that playing hardball is inherently cynical, bereft of virtue, values, or decency, and lies behind the high-profile failures of Enron and others. This is untrue. Hardball does not mean being criminal or even unethical, but it does mean being determined and single-minded.

Wal-Mart became hugely profitable and the biggest retailer in the world by explaining to suppliers exactly how goods should be delivered. Suppliers were given computer information enabling them to track consumer purchases and to help manage inventory, they were told when to resupply Wal-Mart warehouses, and told to deliver only full truck loads at a given time. This system, which is constantly refined, enables Wal-Mart to remove wastage and cost from its supply chain, improving efficiency and margins.

In practice

Hardball has several guiding principles. First, strive for "extreme" competitive advantage. Regulators may worry about market dominance, hardball players do not. Dominance only occurs in extreme situations, and is rightly prevented, but, by trying to dominate, a firm becomes better and actually benefits customers. This links closely with two other points: know the limits to what you can do, and go no further. It is vital that your business is accepted in the markets where you operate, so go as far as possible without alienating customers and communities.

Several key questions will help you decide the limit. Is the action good for the customer? Does it break any laws? Will it directly hurt a competitor? Will it antagonize increasingly influential special interest groups? The right and only answers are, in order: yes, no, no, and no. Serving a customer better than anyone else is vital; targeting a competitor without producing any real benefit for the customer is unnecessary and counter-productive (customers may resent you).

Also important is the need to maintain a relentless focus on competitiveness. This means taking action in two ways. Instill a competitive, customer-focused, entrepreneurial culture, understand what your competitive advantage is – and then exploit it ruthlessly and continually.

Two other points are significant. Use your competitors' weak-nesses to your advantage, but avoid going head to head or competing directly. The danger of direct confrontation is that you will focus too much on competitors at the expense of customers. Finally, develop the right attitudes in yourself and your colleagues. Most people have a natural will to win, so use this. This requires restless impatience, an action-oriented approach, and a desire to change the status quo and constantly improve.

IDEA 94
Web presence

Despite every organization being online, the fundamentals of developing an effective website and presence online are often neglected. The best websites display at least eight out of ten key attributes.

The idea

If your website does ten things well, it will succeed. One organization that has an impressive and varied website with something for everyone is the BBC: www.bbc.co.uk. It focuses on the 10 Cs:

1. Content.

2. Communication.

3. Customer care.

4. Community and culture.

5. Convenience and ease.

6. Connectivity (connecting with other sites and connecting with users).

7. Cost and profitability.

8. Customization.

9. Capability (dynamic, responsive, and flexible).

10. Competitiveness.

In practice

Ten factors exert a significant – often decisive – impact on the success of an organization's online activities. Clearly, some will be more important than others. Some factors are constantly important – notably capability and convenience – whereas other issues assume a greater significance at certain times (for example competitiveness, while always in the background, may assume a sudden and striking importance).

1. *Content*: the need to develop compelling, credible, and customer-focused information. Content needs to be appropriate, add value, stimulate and capture interest, entertain or inform, be accessible and appropriate to the target audience, embody the brand, and above all, engage the customer – ensure that the customer is impressed enough to want to return.

2. *Communication*: the need to engage customers. Customers like to be listened to, and online they expect dialog and interaction.

3. *Customer care*: providing customers with support and confidence. Federal Express took the issue of customer support and turned it into a major source of competitive advantage online. FedEx empowers its customers to find out the status and location of their packages by logging on to its website. This provides support, confidentiality, and ease of use. It also engages customers, by meeting their needs.

4. *Community and culture*: the need for contact and interaction. People like people: they like to interact, and they are essentially

social beings, sharing interests and valuing what they have in common.

5. *Convenience and ease*: the need to make things easier for current and potential customers.

6. *Connectivity*: the need to connect with other sites and users online. The issue of connectivity has two sides. First is the need for users and customers to be connected – physically and emotionally – with your business. Second is the need for sites to connect via a web that actually adds value for the customer and drives traffic for the business.

7. *Cost and profitability*: the need to reduce waste, improve financial efficiency, and drive profits.

8. *Customization*: the value of the internet to supply products and services that are personalized for the customer is vital in a range of industries.

9. *Capability*: the need to ensure that your site remains dynamic, responsive, and flexible.

10. *Competitiveness*: the need to be distinctive.

IDEA 95
Viral marketing

Marketers from many of the largest corporations are using the internet extensively for viral marketing. When Procter & Gamble, GM, Pepsi, and most of the world's largest brands use the internet, it opens the door and reduces the perceived risk.

The idea

The term "viral marketing" was originally invented to describe hotmail.com's email practice of including advertising for itself in outgoing mail from its users. The idea is that if an advertisement reaches a susceptible user, that person will become "infected" (i.e. become a customer or advocate) and can then go on to infect other susceptible users. As long as each infected user contacts more than one susceptible user on average, then the number of infected users will grow fast.

Hotmail.com was developed by Microsoft, and is one of the first free web-based email services. Its strategy is simple. It gives away free email addresses and services with a simple tag at the bottom of every free message: "Get your private, free email at http://www.hotmail.com." People then forward this email to their own network of friends and associates, who see the message and sign up for their own free email service. This then keeps the cycle going, creating an ever-increasing circle of contacts, like a pebble quickly creating ripples in a pond.

In practice

Viral marketing has several key elements:

- *Give away valuable products or services*. Most viral marketing programs give away valuable products or services to attract attention. Viral marketers may not profit immediately, but they know that if they can generate interest from something "free," they will profit soon.

- *Ensure ease of transfer or transmission to others*. Viruses only spread when they are easy to transmit. The medium that carries your marketing message must be easy to transfer and replicate: for example, email, website, or software downloads. Viral marketing works online because instant communication is easy and inexpensive.

- *Provide simplicity*. Marketing messages always work best when they are simple and compelling. Viral marketing messages need to be simple enough to be transmitted easily and without confusion.

- *Exploit people's motivations*. Clever viral marketing campaigns recognize that people want to be connected, cool, popular, or understood. As a result, people produce weblogs and forward emails and web addresses. So, design a marketing strategy that builds on common motivations and behaviors for its transmission.

- *Use existing networks*. People are social, and network marketers have long understood the power of human networks, both the strong, close networks and the weaker networked relationships. Use these networks to communicate your message.

- *Benefit from others' resources*. Creative viral marketing plans use other people's resources to communicate. For example, affiliate programs place text or graphic links on websites, while authors give away free articles or establish weblinks.

IDEA 96
Coaching and supervision

Coaching is a vital leadership skill, and an area of business that has grown dramatically in recent years. The challenge, however, is to ensure that coaches inside and outside the organization are as effective as possible. Supervision provides an important part of the answer.

The idea

Executive coaching is highly effective, increasingly popular, and expensive. The business has grown fast, and inevitably has attracted people who are less than qualified. The challenge, therefore, is to select a coach with the right level of expertise, who will provide a return on the investment. One key element in making this decision is whether the coach is supervised. This involves an experienced expert providing objective and confidential support to the coach.

Supervision is often neglected, yet it is vital for several reasons. If someone supports the coach another perspective is brought to bear, so clients receive two experts for the price of one – especially valuable when faced with complex, intractable issues or difficult choices. Also, by providing feedback, supervision helps ensure quality: an important issue in an industry without regulation where anyone can call themselves an executive coach. In fact, supervision is fast becoming the standard for coaching. The

Association for Professional Executive Coaching and Supervision (APECS), highlights the fact that an increasing number of major corporations now require coaches to be supervised.

A supervisor also contributes to the coach's development, and protects against burn out. A significant hazard among professional coaches is that they will either stray into deep psychological waters with their client, or find themselves psychologically affected by the work and its pressures. A supervisor can help prevent the coach from losing focus or objectivity, and protect them from the inevitable stresses.

It is recommended that a typical coach meet with their supervisor for 90 minutes once every four to six weeks, although this depends on the number of clients and the complexity of the assignment. A supervisor ensures that the coach's relationship with their client is not compromised. Above all, a supervisor makes a qualitative difference to the coach's work. This is hard to quantify, but it undoubtedly improves the coach's effectiveness and the return on investment (RoI). Coaching is expensive, so this qualitative method of improving RoI can be significant.

In practice

- Ask the candidate to coach you for ten minutes. This will give you a real sense of how they work, and also help with the "chemistry test" – a vital step to establishing rapport and building trust.

- Make sure that the coach works from where you are. In other words, they should use whatever tools and processes fit best with your needs.

- Find out the extent of the coach's knowledge of adult learning and behavioral understanding. Remember to be cautious: anyone can claim to be a coach. What models does the coach use? How deep is their coaching expertise?

- Take up the coach's references and assess their experience.

Do they have the right level of practical expertise? What have they achieved, and what else, besides coaching, do they do now?

- Check whether the coach is qualified. There are an increasing number of professional qualifications.

- Finally, go for a coach with a supervisor. This shows that the coach is confident and open, it can help to challenge their perspective, and it provides a measure of reassurance.

IDEA 97
User-centered innovation

If users are encouraged to devise new products and services, innovative new products can be developed quickly in a way that is highly effective and popular. This approached has been championed with great success by the Danish government.

The idea

The first automated drug pumps and heart and lung machines were originally devised by doctors, not medical equipment companies; sports energy drinks were invented by sports enthusiasts before beverage businesses became involved. Increasingly it is users, not producers, who can make the best advances in innovation: inventing, developing, prototyping, and even producing products. Recent research suggests that as much as 70 percent of new product development fails because it does not adequately understand users' needs.

Governments favor innovation because of the economic benefits it provides, and in May 2006 the Danish government announced a national priority of "strengthening user-centered innovation." This policy is pursued by encouraging a wide range of techniques, including research into issues such as ethnography, that enhance understanding of users' needs, directly supporting user-centered innovations, and encouraging Danish business schools and firms to share best practice. According to Danish Minister of Science Helge Sander, the government's focus on user-centered innovation is paying off.

The central theme is to find new, improved ways to connect directly with a shifting group of users when developing new products.

In practice

Good ideas can come from anywhere, and the six Rs approach is especially valuable for identifying opportunities for improvement. Identify something you want to improve, and use the list below to generate ideas.

- *Research*: what can you learn from people or organizations that do this activity well?

- *Reframe*: what is a completely different way of thinking about this?

- *Relate*: what ideas can you borrow from another activity or field?

- *Remove*: what can you eliminate?

- *Redesign*: what can you do to improve this activity, process, or procedure?

- *Rehearse*: what can you do to be certain you have a good idea?

Consider the following actions to identify areas for improvement:

- Talk to people in other areas who deal with similar issues.

- Talk to other companies. Explore how things are done in another industry or country, and think about ideas you can borrow, adapt, or combine.

- Talk to creative people who know nothing about the area but who may have different perspectives.

- Gather a group together to brainstorm ideas.

Finally, it is important to provide a clear focus, otherwise innovation can drift or move in circles. Ensure that innovations are realistic, and plan the implementation of new ideas; innovations often fail because of poor planning or execution.

IDEA 98

Internal promotion and succession planning

Getting succession right is vital. There are two approaches that can be used at different times to ensure success. The internal selection approach advocates choosing successors from within, to ensure a smooth transition, preserve company values, and encourage employees by showing a potential career path. The Darwinian approach favors being open to both internal and external candidates when selecting a successor.

The idea

Organizations struggle with how to turn succession into success. It is necessary to use either internal selection or the Darwinian approach at different levels or at different times. For example, a high percentage (e.g. 80 percent) of senior roles may be internally appointed, while junior roles are selected in a Darwinian way, with employees chosen from a large pool of talent both inside and outside the company. This two-tiered approach is successfully used by many corporations, including HSBC.

The strength of the *Darwinian approach* is that it promotes a meritocratic system, where the most talented workers are selected, bringing fresh perspectives, and increasing the competitiveness of your organization. By choosing influential employees from a diverse array of candidates, a company will gain a valuable range of different skill sets and perspectives to guide it through a variety of challenges. Also, rather than earmarking certain people for possible future promotion, this open approach allows an unrestrained, competitive selection process during succession. If promotion is not guaranteed in advance, all those hoping to be considered for promotion will be motivated to improve business acumen and performance.

Internal promotion involves choosing successors from within an organization, to ensure that people who are already familiar with the company are appointed to leading positions, to ensure consistency and avoid drastic changes. When a seamless transition between key workers is important, internal promotion is useful. It also complements "talent management" and fast-tracking – where certain employees are marked for possible future promotion. These are powerful motivators. Running against "best practice" guidelines prevailing in the UK at the time, internal promotion was favored by HSBC when Sir John Bond left his position as chairman in 2006 to be replaced by CEO Stephen Green. This ensured the new chairman would be familiar with the organization, and that other employees would know what to expect.

In practice

Internal promotion:

■ Find ways of motivating workers who are not interested in promotion. Although "fast-tracking" can help retain certain workers interested in corporate advancement, there are often a number of valuable employees who do not desire such promotions.

- Recognize that internal promotion may not be the best option when an organization is underperforming or when significant changes need to be made.

- Prepare employees who are earmarked for promotion for the jobs they will take over. A benefit of internal succession plans is that individuals can be groomed beforehand for the new responsibilities they will take on.

- Ensure workers at the top do not feel threatened by succession plans. This can have demotivating and negative results for everyone involved in the process.

Darwinian succession:

- Bring in external talent as part of the succession process to revitalize a failing company.

- If there is little variety in your organization, recruiting from outside your organization can widen your "corporate gene pool."

- When selecting a successor, utilize a range of advice and opinions from experts inside and outside the organization.

IDEA 99
Developing knowledge and intellectual capital

Developing intellectual capital is imperative, as knowledge is an asset and a source of power. As Lew Platt, former CEO of Hewlett Packard, says: "If HP knew what it knows, we would be three times as profitable."

The idea

Knowledge is the intellectual capital that an organization possesses. Technological developments and the internet have promoted an explosion in the scope and depth of available knowledge. As there is so much information and knowledge available, it is important for organizations to know how to creatively develop and use information.

Intellectual capital is an asset that is created from knowledge. As writer Thomas Stewart argues, "Intelligence becomes an asset when some useful order is created out of free-flowing brainpower ... organizational intellect becomes intellectual capital only when it can be deployed to do something that could not be done if it remained scattered round like so many coins in the gutter."

Knowledge and information have to be collected, protected, and effectively managed if they are to be valuable resources.

Appointed in 1991 as the world's first director of intellectual capital at Skandia (Sweden's largest financial services corporation), Leif Edvinsson divided intellectual capital into three types:

- Human capital, in the heads of employees.

- Structural capital, which remains in the organization.

- Customer capital, deriving from the relationships that the company enjoys with its customers. Customer capital is often seen as a subset of structural capital.

Skandia's measures track whether intellectual capital is increasing or decreasing, focusing the organization's culture and thinking on increasing its intangible asset. In Edvinsson's view:

> Intellectual capital is a combination of human capital – the brains, skills, insights and potential of those in an organization – and structural capital – things like the processes wrapped up in customers, processes, databases, brands and systems. It is the ability to transform knowledge and intangible assets into wealth-creating resources, by multiplying human capital with structural capital. This is the intellectual capital multiplier effect.

At Skandia, human capital is divided into customer focus, process focus, and renewal and development focus. Edvinsson designed a process for each business unit to report on all areas of intellectual capital, enabling the organization to quantify its intangible intellectual capital assets. Moreover, managing intellectual capital has nurtured innovation and new thinking, and has helped create a mindset that will enable Skandia to compete in the future.

In practice

- *Undertake a knowledge audit.* Few firms know what knowledge they possess – because knowledge is confined to a few, or simply neglected. A knowledge audit will uncover the breadth, depth, and location of an organization's knowledge. It has three core components:

- Define what knowledge assets exist – especially information or skills that are difficult or expensive to replace.
- Locate the assets: who keeps or "owns" them.
- Classify them, and assess how they relate to other assets. This will reveal opportunities in other parts of the organization.

■ *Increase knowledge in key areas*. This can be done in three ways: it can be bought, rented (e.g. by hiring consultants), or developed through training.

■ *Maintain knowledge*. Knowledge gaps make an organization more vulnerable to competition. Lost expertise and experience following "downsizing," and the erosion of traditional employee loyalty, highlight the urgent need to capture, codify, and store people's expertise and tacit knowledge.

■ *Protect knowledge*. Explicit knowledge, such as copyright or information codified in handbooks, systems, or procedures, can be legally protected. Tacit knowledge, information retained by individuals, including learning, experience, observation, deduction, and informally acquired knowledge, can only enjoy limited legal protection through, for example, non-compete clauses. It is necessary to ensure that valuable tacit knowledge is recorded and passed on.

■ *Establish information systems*. An efficient information management system will coordinate and control information, and help with planning. When developing a system, decide what information is needed to help improve decisions and achieve objectives.

■ *Manage the flow of information*. Understand how information flows, what it is used for, and the ways in which it can be applied.

IDEA 100
Decision making and the paradox of choice

In this last section we consider how great ideas and decisions are made, how bad ones are avoided, and the one fact that unites them all – the human mind.

The idea

Paradoxically, the more choices you have, the tougher life can be. This is because greater choice comes at a price: potentially more time, demands on your cognitive abilities, and confusion and paralysis resulting from indecision. Decision making is central to business success and generating new ideas, yet it is littered with hazards. Understanding the pitfalls is half the story; trusting yourself is the other.

In practice

The way that people think, both as individuals and collectively, affects the decisions they make, in ways that are far from obvious and rarely understood. John S. Hammond, Ralph L. Keeney, and Howard Raiffa recognized the following traps in decision making (see "The hidden traps in decision-making," *Harvard Business Review*, September–October 1998).

- *The anchoring trap* is where we give disproportionate weight to the first piece of information we receive. The initial impact of the first information, our immediate reaction to it, is so significant that it outweighs everything else, "drowning" our ability to evaluate a situation.

- *The status quo trap* biases us towards maintaining the current situation – even when better alternatives exist – due to inertia or the potential loss of face if the current position was to change.

- *The sunk-cost trap* inclines us to perpetuate the mistakes of the past, because the investment involved makes abandonment of previous decisions unthinkable.

- *The confirming evidence trap* (confirmation bias) is when we seek information to support an existing position, to discount opposing information, to justify past decisions, and to support the continuation of the current favored strategy.

- *The over-confidence trap* makes us overestimate the accuracy of our forecasts. Linked to confirming evidence, it occurs when a decision maker has an exaggerated belief in their ability to understand situations and predict the future.

- *The framing trap* is when a problem or situation is incorrectly stated, undermining the decision-making process. This is often but not always unintentional. How an issue or situation is seen is important in providing the basis for developing an effective strategy or decision.

- *The recent event trap* leads us to give undue weight to a recent, possibly dramatic, event or sequence of events. It is similar to the anchoring trap, except that it can arise at any time – not just at the start – and cause misjudgment.

- *The prudence trap* leads us to be over-cautious when estimating uncertain factors. There is a tendency to be very risk averse, and is likely to occur when there is a decision dilemma – when the decision maker feels that both the current approach and alternative courses carry risks.

As well as these thinking flaws and coping patterns, there are two potential pitfalls resulting from the culture or environment of the organization: fragmentation and groupthink.

Fragmentation occurs when people are in disagreement with either their peers or their superiors. Usually the expression of emerging dissent is disguised or suppressed, although it may appear as "passive aggression." Dissenting opinion often festers in the background – mentioned informally in conversation, rather than clearly raised in formal situations, such as meetings. Fragmentation is corrosive, hindering effective analysis and decision making, and can worsen when the views of one group dominate. It also feeds off itself in a self-sustaining cycle, as any move to break it is seen as an attempt to gain dominance by one side. It can therefore become locked in to the organization, and be extremely difficult to reverse.

Groupthink is the opposite of fragmentation. It occurs when the group suppresses ideas that are critical or not in support of the direction in which it is moving. The group appears to be in agreement or certain, but is neither. It is caused by many factors, such as past success breeding a belief of an infallible team, and complacency. Groupthink may occur because members of the group are denied information, or lack the confidence or ability to challenge the dominant views of the group. People may be concerned about disagreeing because of past events, present concerns, or a fear of what the future might hold, and therefore seek safety in numbers.

Groupthink is exacerbated by the fact that cohesive groups tend to rationalize the invulnerability of their decision or strategy, and this in turn inhibits critical analysis and the expression of dissenting ideas. The effect is an incomplete survey of available options, and a failure to examine the risks of preferred decisions.

Groupthink can occur in organizations where teamwork is either strong or weak. As with fragmentation, groupthink is self-sustaining. The longer it lasts, the more entrenched and "normal" it becomes. It can be very difficult to reverse.

Now we have explained the pitfalls, what are the solutions? A great deal has been written about the rational, process-driven approach to decision making, but the psychological aspects are also important, and are only recently beginning to be understood:

■ *Be bold and don't fear the consequences of decisions.* We tend to over-estimate the consequences, good and bad, of our choices. We also tend to discount our ability to make the right choice. This results from "loss aversion": the view that a loss will hurt more than a gain will please. Remember, the worst-case scenario might never occur, and even if it does, people invariably have the psychological resilience to cope.

■ *Trust your instincts and emotions.* We have evolved to make good decisions and manage their implementation. Sometimes, quick decisions work best precisely because you have picked up on the key pieces of information quickly and then responded. More time can simply lead to information overload and other distractions.

■ *Be prepared to play devil's advocate.* Searching for flaws and failings will strengthen your decisions, and illuminate factors affecting the decision and other issues, such as biases. This means being aware of confirmation bias and using it.

■ *Avoid irrelevancies.* Irrelevant information distorts our perception, as described in the anchoring trap. The solution is to be ready to question the context of the information. What are you basing your decision on, and is it really relevant?

■ *Reframe the decision.* This will help you view the issues from a new perspective.

■ *Don't let the past hold you back.* The sunk-cost trap high-lights our tendency to stick with previous choices because too much has been invested for a change to be acceptable. Don't: better alternatives may exist.

- *Challenge groupthink*. People are often afraid to comment or to act because of social pressure. This is a poor excuse. Find out what people really think, and use that to inform decisions.

- *Limit your options*. This is the paradox of choice: the more options we have, the harder life can be. Choose the most promising options. This can help to remove pressure and clarify your thinking. We are fixated with choices, believing more to be better. In truth, less choice can be more satisfying. Also, it may be worth delegating the decision to someone else better qualified.

The challenge is to make sure that, as far as possible, you enjoy what you are doing, and that the decision is made by the best person, in the right way at the right time.

Now there's an idea.

Bibliography

Bibb, Sally; Kourdi, Jeremy (2007) *A Question of Trust: The crucial nature of trust in business, work and life - and how to build it*, Cyan Books.

Charan, Ram; Drotter, Stephen; Noel, James (2001) *The Leadership Pipeline: How to build the leadership-powered company*, Jossey-Bass.

De Bono, Edward (2000) *Six Thinking Hats*, Penguin Books.

Diamond, Jared M.(2005) *Guns, Germs and Steel: A short history of everybody for the last 13,000 years*, Vintage.

Gladwell, Malcolm (2002) *The Tipping Point*, Abacus.

Goleman, Daniel (1996) *Emotional Intelligence: Why it can matter more than IQ*, Bloomsbury Publishing.

Hammer, Michael; Champy, James (2001) *Reengineering the Corporation: A manifesto for business revolution*, Nicholas Brealey Publishing.

Kanter, Rosabeth Moss (1998) *The Change Masters*, Jossey Bass Wiley.

Kaplan, Robert S.; Norton, David P. (1996) *Balanced Scorecard: Translating strategy into action*, Harvard Business School Press.

Kelley, Tom; Littman, Jonathan (2001) *The Art of Innovation: Lessons in creativity from Ideo, America's leading design firm*, Currency.

Kim, Chan W.; Mauborgne, Renée (2005) *Blue Ocean Strategy:*

How to create uncontested market space and make the competition irrelevant, Harvard Business School Press.

Kotter, John P. (1996) *Leading Change*, Harvard Business School Press.

Lachenauer, R; MacMillan, Ian C.; van Putten, Alexander B.; Gunther McGrath, Rita; Stalk, George Jr. (2006) "Hardball Strategies", *Harvard Business Review*, September.

Marchand, Donald A.; Kettinger, William; Rollins, John D. (2001) *Making the Invisible Visible: How companies win with the right information, people and IT*, Wiley and Sons.

McGrath, Rita Gunther; MacMillan, Ian C. (2005) *MarketBusters: 40 strategic moves that drive exceptional business growth*, Harvard Business School Press.

Moore, Geoffrey A. (1998) *Inside the Tornado: Marketing strategies from Silicon Valley's cutting edge*, Capstone Publishing.

Sebenius, James K. (2001) "Six Habits of Merely Effective Negotiators", *Harvard Business Review*, April.

Senge, Peter (2006) *The Fifth Discipline*, Random House Business Books.

Stewart, Thomas A. (1998) *Intellectual Capital: The new wealth of organizations*, Nicholas Brealey Publishing.

Warren, Kim (2002) *Competitive Strategy Dynamics*, John Wiley and Sons.

Warren, Kim (2003) *The Critical Path: Building performance into the future*, Vola Press.

ISBN 978-1-905736-08-9

£8.99 paperback